From The Pigpen To The Pulpit & Beyond

From The Pigpen To The Pulpit & Beyond

Eddie Watson D-Min

XULON PRESS

Xulon Press
2301 Lucien Way #415
Maitland, FL 32751
407.339.4217
www.xulonpress.com

Other references: The Broadman Hymnal, 1940, The Broadman Press; The Baptist Hymnal, 1991, Convention Press; William Fay & Ralph Hodge, Share Jesus Without Fear, Life Way Press; E.C. Mckenzie, 14,000 Quips and Quotes, Hendrickson Publishers; James Strong, LL.D., S.T.D., The New Strong's Exhaustive Concordance of the Bible; Dr. Billy Graham, Angels, Word Publishing

For more information concerning speaking engagements or revivals contact:

Eddie Watson at 728 Days Ave., Morris, Ga. 39867
or
by phone at (229) 768-2820
or
229-308-9467

e-mail address – eddiewatson@windstream.net

Paperback ISBN-13: 978-1-6628-4991-6
eBook ISBN-13: 978-1-6628-4992-3

This book is dedicated first and foremost to the glory of God!
Without him I could do nothing!

And to my parents, E.E. (Red) & Bernice (Winkie) Watson for their love and support! It helped me become who I am today!

To the wife God provided for me – Tammie
and the family God blessed me with!

And to my Church family that has provided strength and encouragement during this journey! This family reaches far beyond Clay Hill where I have been blessed to Pastor. It reaches to all my brothers and sisters in Christ that have ministered to me or allowed me to have the privilege to minister to them
And
To my Emmaus Family!

Thank you all for your inspiration!

Acknowledgments

I thank God for loving me and not giving up on me even when I was in a far country. I thank Jesus Christ for loving me enough to give his life as a payment for my sin. I thank the Holy Spirit for bringing me under conviction so that I could repent and turn back to God, and for giving me the ability to do things for the Lord that are 'way beyond" my natural ability.

I thank my father and mother for starting me off on the right track. Even though I have wandered outside of my lane, at least I did know where the finish line was. I also thank my mother for naming this book and for the encouragement that she gave me to write it.

I thank my in-laws for all their love and support. Jimmie and Shirley, I wouldn't trade you for anything.

I thank Andy Bryan, Jeff Hines, Randy Stokes, Mike Lee, Bill Sanders, Billy Starling, Ed Holloway, and Dr. and Mrs. Vonn Johnson for your inspiration, encouragement, support, and friendship. Some of you may find some things in this book that you recall saying.

A special thanks to Jo Anna Giles for helping this ole suthun cuntry hick wiff his gramma an spellin. I couldn't have done it without you. Thank you to Jeff Hines for going over the re-write.

I thank Nan Stanfield for sharing her God given gift with me by writing a poem for my ordination service and as a foreword for this book.

Foreword
By Nan Stanfield

I sat in my newfound Church one Sunday morning, not really knowing most of the people sitting around me. I knew only one thing for sure; that God had sent me there to find the love and fellowship I had needed for so long. A young man in cowboy boots and jeans rose from his seat and stood before us holding a microphone. When the music started he closed his eyes and sang with one of the most beautiful voices I had ever heard. I thought to myself, "this magnificent voice could make a million in country music". Right then and there; God spoke to my spirit, "This one is mine," He said; "I will do great things with Him, if He will allow it."

I knew very little about Eddie at the time, but soon learned that he came from a long line of farming folk. His parents, his wife and daughter, were no strangers to hard work. They raised crops and some of the finest hogs in the area. Their operation was so big that some men in the church would help with bringing in the crops, and loading the hogs for market, etc.

As my knowledge of these wonderful people grew, so did my love and respect for them. He and his family were hard workers in the church as well. Privileged to watch them grow in their Christian commitment and love of the Lord, I still felt that God had something special in mind for Eddie. They were often in my mind and always in my prayers. What a joy I felt, the day I heard him announce that "God had called him into His Ministry." The poem on the following page was presented to Eddie at his Ordination Service.

IN COWBOY BOOTS & JEANS

By Nan Stanfield

You could have sought your fortune
Through earthly wealth and fame,
You had the voice, You had the looks,
But then God called out your name.

You have chosen to follow Jesus,
And we thank you for that choice,
For it matters not what could have been,
But that you listened to God's voice.

As Peter went from a fisherman
Then through Christ to a fisher of men,
So you go from the harvest of the land,
To the harvest of souls for him.

You prepared the soil and planted the seed
And you know what hard work means
Now you're ready to be God's messenger
In cowboy boots and jeans.

Introduction

When I wrote the original book "From the Pigpen to the Pulpit" over 20 years ago, I started with the knowledge that what I was about to undertake was, in reality way beyond my natural ability. I never really liked school, and I certainly never liked writing. I barely scraped through my years at Clay County High School, and the pattern was the same during my two years at Abraham Baldwin Agricultural College. I speak "suthun" slang, my grammar is terrible; and I have never understood algebra since the first day I walked into the classroom.

My family raised purebred hogs for as long as I can remember. When you are around something all your life, you really learn a lot about it. I have judged hogs, shown hogs, clipped hogs, washed hogs, groomed hogs, fed hogs, watered hogs, sorted hogs, cut hogs, given injections to hogs, ear notched hogs, operated on hogs, performed autopsies on hogs, assisted in breeding hogs, assisted in farrowing hogs, artificially bred hogs, collected, extended, and sold semen from hogs. I have kept records on hogs; I have bought hogs, sold hogs, comforted hogs, pushed hogs, kicked hogs, and whipped hogs. I have put up hog fences, built hog catch-pens, hog sheds, hog barns, hog nurseries, and hog parlors. I have cleaned hog pens by scraping, shoveling, washing, pressure washing and disinfecting. I have been literally in contact at some time with every part of a hog, inside and out. There are a lot of things I do not know, but I do know hogs! You could say that I have spent much of my life literally in the pigpen.

One day I realized that not only had I spent much of my life in the literal pigpen, but I had been in the spiritual pigpen as well. When I started the original book, I was still entering the literal pigpen most everyday, but thank God, I was no longer in the spiritual one. Thanks to the conviction of the Holy Spirit and the power of God drawing me, I was able to step out in faith from the spiritual pigpen and receive blessings from God that were beyond my imagination. How could a guy who knows nothing about music be able to write, sing, and record songs? How could a man whose voice would crack, and knees would shake when talking about his Lord and Savior now proclaim the gospel of Jesus Christ boldly? How could a guy who never really liked school earn a Doctorate Degree in Christian Ministry (with good grades)? How could a redneck, poor, dirt, hog farmer write a book and since go on to write more? There is only one explanation. It could only happen through the power and blessings of God! *"Try me now in this, " says the Lord of hosts, "if I will not open for you the windows of heaven and pour out for you such blessing that there will not be room enough to receive it."* (Mal. 3:10)

People of this world tend to judge others on their past or where they have been. I have been in the spiritual pigpen, which is equivalent to a spiritual cesspool. I am thankful that Jesus in not interested in my past; he is concerned more with my future. He does not care where I have been, but he cares where I am going. Sometimes it is hard for religious people to see where you are going because they are too busy looking at where you have been. For the Bible tells us, *"Therefore, if anyone is in Christ, he is a new creation; old things have passed away; behold, all things have become new."* (2Cor. 5:17) What I was, where I have been, and what I have done passed away when I submitted my life to Jesus Christ. God at that moment, made all things new. Do not judge a person today by what he was or what he did before coming to know Jesus. God does not operate that way, and if you claim to be his, why should you? It is much easier for me to relate to a person who admits he has been in the pigpen that one who has not. It is hard for someone to explain the grace of God to me when they act as if they have never sinned. If you really want to know about the grace of God you need to hear it from someone who has experienced it first-hand. Sharing our testimony of Christ with others is God's way of spreading the gospel; so do not get upset when a dirty, rotten sinner develops a sparkle in his eye, as song in his heart, and praise of God on his lips. He may have had hands-on experience with God's grace—the grace that you have only heard about. Listen and learn from my experience.

When the original "From the Pigpen to the Pulpit" was written, I used language and lingo that was well versed by those inside the church. Over the years I have discovered that there are people outside the church who do not truly understand the language of the church which could have caused misunderstandings. I have also discovered that many church members use churchy language that they themselves do not fully comprehend. In this book, I hope to have simplified, or given better explanation to some of the words used as well as make additions in hope that those who read will have an even better understanding of the grace of God and the way of salvation. There is no blanket salvation policy that covers everyone. There is no secret prayer that you give or ritual that you perform. You can't just apologize to God, and continue living your life as you please. It is all about getting to know the one who sacrificed His life for yours. It is about answering His call. It is about trusting Him enough to live your life for Him. It is about following Jesus! It is about discipleship! Anything less does not qualify for God's saving grace. Anything less is cheap grace, given by sinful men which will be useless when you leave this world.

This book was not written to judge or condemn anyone. It was written to give you insight into your own life and hope for your future. Like Jesus, I am not concerned with where you have been or where you are now. I am concerned with where you are going. I hope you are going with me. I am headed toward home, my heavenly home. Jesus said, *I go to prepare a place for you. And if I go and prepare a place for you, I will come again and receive you to myself; that where I m there you may be also.*" (John 14:2-3)

Chapter 1

Luke 15: 11-12 Then He said: "A certain man had two sons. And the younger of them said to his father, 'Father, give me the portion of goods that falls to me.' So he divided to them his livelihood."

Many times, when you think of this parable of the prodigal son, someone will come to your mind (ole Joe down the street) who has wandered away from God and lived a backslidden life. You may have even seen a miraculous change in ole Joe's life and now see him living a full Christian life. Maybe he has not made that change, but as you read these verses, they offer a prayer and hope that one day the change will come.

It is easy to recognize the parallel of other people's lives in this story, but what about our own lives? A number of years ago, as I stood outside the church visiting, a gentleman came up and shook my hand and told me that he was praying for me. At this time in my life, I really thought I was a pretty good fellow. My first thoughts were: "Why are you praying for me? I'm okay. There's nothing wrong with me; I don't need your prayers. What's your problem?" Of course I did not tell him that, but those thoughts were racing around in my head. It was not until almost two years later that I realized just how desperately I did need his prayers because I had not been truly trusting Jesus as I should. It is amazing how a person's attitude about prayer changes when God finally gets a grip on them. God changed my life, and I thanked the gentleman publicly for his prayers. Thanks again, Mike. Keep praying, because I still need it; and now I covet the prayers of my fellow brothers and sisters in Christ. You see, if we were truthful to ourselves, we would not have to look down the street but into our own hearts and lives in order to find that rebellious son.

The father in this story represents God, and the rebellious son, you guessed it, us. Before you vocalize your denial, read on. Being a daddy myself, I can imagine what this father must have been going through and the hurt he must have felt as his son seemed more interested in what the father had to offer in terms of material possessions than in desiring fellowship with him. We say, "Surely, this can't be me!" How many times have we put work or play before worship attendance? We say this one time will not matter. Then once becomes twice and three times, and our next excuse is that we have just gotten out of the habit of going to church. I am afraid that a habit is all it is to many people. God has been called many things by his children: my Lord, Master, Savior, Redeemer, and Friend. "My habit" just does not have the same ring to it, and I am quite sure that my heavenly Father does not think much of it either. The question is, "If he is your habit, is he really your heavenly Father?" I would hate to leave this world with that question on my mind. If he is not your heavenly Father, then one day when you stand before God (and you will) he will say, "I *never knew you; depart from me you who practice lawlessness*! " (Mat. 7:23) The problem with most people today is that they know <u>of God</u> instead of knowing God. There is a difference! Many people know about God; they know the facts about God, but they do not know him personally. They do not have a relationship with him. They do not talk with him daily, read his word, or listen for that "*still small voice*," (1 Kings 19:12) with which God speaks to us. They may know him with their head, but they do not know him with their hearts. Someone once said that many professing Christians are only eighteen inches away from heaven. That is about the distance from your head to your heart. Jesus warned the Scribes and Pharisees about having mouth-action knowledge of God. *These people draw near to me with their mouth, and honor me with their lips, but their heart is far from me.* (Mat. 15:8) The Bible says, "*Seek ye first the kingdom of God and his righteousness, and all these things will be added to you.*" (Mat. 6:33) All too often seeking God is last on our list instead of first.

We never forget to ask our school children if they have done their homework, but how many times do we ask, "Have you read God's word or talked to your heavenly Father today?" We seem to be so concerned with our children's future, but are we? The things that matter most, we neglect. We try to prepare our kids for the next fifty years, and yet we have little concern for eternity. We stress to our children the importance of being successful and preparing for retirement on this earth. In recent days parents aren't even worried about business, success, or retirement. Their thought process is more like - my son or daughter is going to be a super star athlete! They lay aside everything for sports and the kids do it all! Baseball, basketball, football!!! League ball, travel ball, tournament play! It's all in for everything... Except God! We just don't have time for church; my child has ball games on Sunday and Wednesday's! Or maybe it is just practice... but we gotta go or they won't let my kid play! If every parent was as concerned about their child's spiritual life as they were about sports there wouldn't be a game or practice on Sunday's or Wednesday's! 26% of parents whose children play high school sports hope their child will become a professional athlete one day. Among families with household incomes of less than $50,000 annually, the number is 39%. According to the National Collegiate Athletic Association, only 1 in 168 high school baseball players will get drafted by a Major League Baseball team. That is less than.6%! My personal feelings are that those statistics are a bit high. Only 1 in 2,451 boy's high school basketball players will get drafted by a National Basketball Association team. That is 04%! Now let us look at some other odds. There is 100% chance your child will die and there is a 100% chance he will stand before Jesus to give an account of his life. *They will give an account to Him who is ready to judge the living and the dead* (1 Pet. 4:5) *For the Father judges no one, but has committed all judgment to the Son* (John 5:22) With those statistics, what should you really be more concerned about! Should we not be more concerned about preparing our children spiritually? Is it not even more important to be led by the Holy Spirit? *For as many as are led by the spirit of God, these are the sons of God.* (Rom. 8:14) After all, what is better than being a child of God and having a heavenly Father who owns it all?

How many times when we pray to God, do we ask for something? Do we ever just take the time to thank God for his presence in our lives, express a desire just to be closer to him, or just bask in his glory? More times than not we are asking for something. All too often we call out to God to help us out of a predicament we find ourselves in. When we are about to lose a loved one from sickness or an accident, we plead with God. Leaning over the commode hurling, we promise God we will never drink again if we live. The problem is, we do; we live, and we drink again. A teenage couple goes too far and prays to God that they are too young to have a child. Someone has a one-night stand with someone they do not know, and cries out to God, "Please don't let me have aids." We soon find out that sin has its consequences, some that we may have to live with for the rest of our lives. If we had only listened to our heavenly Father and followed him, we would not be in this mess; but we just had to do it our way.

Asking is not always bad. After all, the Bible says, "Y*e have not because ye ask not*." (James 4:2) A father does love to give his children gifts, and God is the best gift giver of all. (Mat. 7:11) Our problem is not really the asking, but the attitude. We have the attitude that we want this and we want it now, whether it is what we need or not. Even if we do not vocalize our feelings, it is in our hearts. The Bible says in Luke 16:15 that God knows our heart. He not only knows our heart, but he knows all about us. After all, the Bible teaches us in Isaiah 44:24 that he formed us from the womb. God knows our strengths and our weaknesses. He knows what is best for us, but he will allow us to make our own choices, even though it may break his heart.

Often our choices will leave us broken-hearted as well. If we truly belong to God, if we are really his children, then we cannot be truly happy outside of his will. We can try our hardest to run from God and say that we are going to live our own lives, but something will always be missing. There will be a yearning that we cannot understand, an emptiness that we cannot seem to fill. It is only when we draw close to the Lord and follow him that we find true joy and fulfillment in life. Jesus said, "*I have come that they might have life and that they might have it more abundantly*." (John 10:10) It is God's desire for us to follow Christ and for us to allow Christ to live in and through us. If we follow Christ, we will be living in God's will, and God will be close to us; for Jesus said, "*I and my father are one*." *(John 10:30)* God has everything we need to have abundant life. If we stay close to him, it is available to us, just as the son in this scripture had everything available to him in his father's home. In verse 31 of the fifteenth chapter of Luke, we see this when the father talked to his other son as he told him, "A*ll that I have is yours.*" If we really want what the father has, all we have to do is stay in his presence. *Draw nigh to God and he will* *draw nigh to you.* (James 4:8) It is much easier to stay in Gods' will when we are in his presence and talk with him daily.

God has a plan for our lives just as I am sure the father in the parable had dreams for his son. We all want our children to have the good things in life. We certainly would not want them to suffer or be in need. Our desire as a parent is to nurture, provide, and protect them. We know the father loved his son, and he, no doubt, provided for his every need. When we as parents try to protect our children, they sometimes see it only as restrictions. They want to be free to do their own thing. What they fail to realize is that with freedom comes responsibility. That is usually the thing they want no part of, but a good parent knows freedom without responsibility is trouble. When a child is living at home, there is a relationship. There is dialog (or at least there should be) between the father and son. There is some stability and guidance. There comes a time in every parent's life when they must let their children make decisions for themselves, and it breaks their hearts to see their child heading down the wrong path. Some people, young and old, just will not listen to reason. There are some lessons we only learn by experience, although that is not the way our heavenly Father would prefer that we learn them. He wants to prevent us from having those difficulties in life, and he would if we would only follow him. Being the loving Father he is, he will not force his will on us. He just waits patiently for us to ask, just as his only begotten son prayed, "*Not my will but thine be done.*" (Luke 22:42)

The son in this parable was not satisfied with the father taking care of the little details in his life. I am sure he probably had not even thought of many of these details that his father had been taking care of for years, such as food, clothing, and shelter. Nowadays the list would be even larger and would include things like light bills, water bills, insurance, and, do not forget those telephone bills. (If you have a teenager in the house you know what I mean.) Now, it is not only cell phones, but smart phones with unlimited talk, text, internet access, and every app known to mankind! It can't be any phone... It has to be the latest and greatest! There are also those other necessities such as CD's, remote control batteries, and now Bluetooth headsets. It is amazing what used to be thought of as extravagances have now become necessities.

The son may have felt that he was being held back. He may have had ideas that were rejected at home such as a new catch-pen design for the cattle, or a new corn variety that JSU (Jerusalem State University) had success with in its field trials. Although it is hard for us to see, many times the father may be keeping us out of real trouble.

God finds ways all during the day to remind us that he will guide our paths if we would but follow him. I have spent many hours on a tractor. In recent years I have used this time in prayer and meditation. Some jobs are easy, while others require your undivided attention. Bedding land and laying off rows are jobs that need to be done with accuracy. Rows that are too wide mean weeds in the middles; rows that are too narrow mean no room for the cultivator, and the corn will be plowed up. One day while on this particular job, I found myself in my own little world. I was talking to God. I had become oblivious to all that was around me or what I was doing. I had been in this state for an hour or more when something brought me back to earth. I had an anxious moment when I realized what a mess I could have made, but as I reached the end of the row and looked back, the row was perfectly straight. Being the conscientious fellow that I am, I said to myself, "Self, you gotta pay attention to whatchew - a - doin r u gonna be done made yo-sef a mess." (Sorry, that's just the way us redneck hog farmer plow hands talk.) So any way, I really kept my eyes on the row mark; I was watching it closely, concentrating hard, trying to keep the row straight. When I reached the other end and looked back, the row looked like a rattlesnake track. Crooked was an understatement. At that moment, God spoke to my heart and said," Son, keep your eyes focused on me, and I will take care of the details in your life." Sounds like a pretty good deal to me, how about you?

You may ask, "How can I be sure that the Lord will be there for me?" You can be sure because of the promise Jesus made when he said, "I *will never leave thee, nor forsake thee.*" (Heb. 13:5) *So we may boldly say," The Lord is my helper* ". (Heb. 13:6) All we have to do to have God's guidance and help is to believe in the Lord Jesus Christ and follow him. God has already taken care of the most difficult problem in your life when he sent Jesus to bear the cross of Calvary for payment of your sin, so that by faith in him you can become his child. Just accept what God has already done for you and step out in faith and let God take control; for "*we are to walk by faith, not by sight.*" (2 Cor. 5:7)

Before you go any farther, ask yourself, "Have I really accepted what Jesus did at Calvary as payment for my sin?" and if so, "Am I following him daily or do I only call on him when I am in need?" What kind of child am I, wise or rebellious? Now think of the consequences. *Rebuke is more effective for a wise man than a hundred blows on a fool. An evil man seeks only rebellion; therefore a cruel messenger will be sent against him.* (Prov. 17:10-11) Although it may seem harsh when God rebukes or chastises us, it is surely better to repent and turn back to the Lord than to allow more harm to come our way. Where do you stand with the Lord? Are you following him daily, or are you going your own way? You think that even though you do not spend much time with God, he must be pleased with you because your life seems to be going ok. Do not be too sure; if you are truly his child, then he will only let you go so far before he allows things to crumble around you. He will do this to bring you back to him. Remember, when things start to go wrong and seem to be headed down a dead-end street, do not just pass it off and say, "That's life." It may be just life, or it may be a life without God. Think about it. Have you talked to him lately? He wants to hear from you.

Chapter 2

LUKE 15:13 AND NOT MANY DAYS AFTER, THE YOUNGER SON GATHERED ALL TOGETHER, AND JOURNEYED TO A FAR COUNTRY, AND THERE WASTED HIS POSSESSIONS WITH PRODIGAL LIVING.

The younger son journeyed to a far country. The Greek word used here for *country* is *chora*, pronounced *kho-rah*. Its base is from the word *chasma,* meaning chasm or vacancy; therefore, we have the idea of empty expanse. Life without feeling the closeness and presence of God is just that, empty; but there are times when that is hard to see. You know the grass is always greener on the other side of the fence. After you have jumped several fences in search of greener pastures, you realize the true meaning of the saying, "The grass is always greener over the septic tank." It is plush on the surface, but underneath it is just, uh, well, uh, you know what I mean.

If you had grown up on a farm as this son that we know as the prodigal son did, you would have to work. The work had become a drudgery to him. I am sure he noticed that the guys who lived in town did not have to work as hard and as long as he did. His gaze over the fence at what seemed like greener pastures was the sin, "*Thou shalt not covet,*" (Exodus 20:17) that led to his restlessness. Instead of being grateful and thankful for the things that the father provided, he coveted the life of ease, prosperity, and luxury. These things have not only brought down many people, but they have brought down many nations as well. Prosperity, many times, leads people to become dependent on oneself instead of God. The farther away one gets from God, the closer one comes to destruction. The destruction is caused from pride. When pride takes control of a person, he feels that he can handle everything on his own; he no longer needs Gods help. God's word tells us different. *Pride goes before destruction, and a haughty spirit before a fall.* (Prov. 16:18) For some reason, human foresight is virtually non-existent when it comes to our desires. Our motto has become "Give me the easy life, and give it to me now." Jesus said, "*Take heed and beware of covetousness, for one's life does not consist in the abundance of the things he possesses.*" (Luke 12:15) Jesus also told a parable about a rich man who decided to pull down his old barns and build new barns so he could store up his goods and relax and take life easy. God was not impressed by this and required his soul that very night. In other words, he croaked; he bit the dust; he kicked the bucket; his wick went out; he crashed; he died. Jesus said, "*He who lays up treasure for himself, is not rich toward God.*" (Luke 12:21) The son in this parable did not lay up treasure for himself because he thought his father had laid up enough that he did not have to worry; and he would not have, had he been living in line with God's will. The Bible says he wasted it on prodigal living. The King James Version calls it "riotous living." The Greek word here is *asotos,* which means wildly extravagant and grossly self-indulgent spending, lacking restraint, and loose in morals. There is no doubt he had never heard the saying, "You won't continue having a horn of plenty if you keep blowing it." It almost sounds just like another day in good old USA or Washington, DC, for sure.

The King James Version of the Bible says the son wasted his substance. The word *substance* in the dictionary has more meanings than just possessions, and in this we find a deeper meaning to God's word. One of the definitions to the word *substance* is the ultimate reality that underlies all outward manifestation and change. This means he lost that reality that he was a son of the father, and in doing so his life's decisions were not a manifestation of the father. To put it plain and simple, he did not act like his daddy, and his father's influence was no longer known in his life. When children start to go over fools' hill, or sow wild oats, you hear their parents say, "Well, they certainly were not raised that way." In this perspective, they have lost their substance.

The son in this parable had reached the age of decision. When you decide to turn away from God, remember, he will not force you to stay although he knows it would be in your best interest if you would.

Another problem he had to deal with was peer pressure, and as the saying goes, "I've been there, done that." When my cousin and I went over fools' hill, I might not have been driving, but I am sure I was giving directions. It is amazing how miserable people can fool others into believing that they are having a wonderful time. They drink and use drugs to cover up the fact that they are lonely, afraid, or hurting. To those who are searching for greener pastures, it all appears to be one huge party—no worries, no hassle, just let the good times roll. They are blinded to the fact that when the lights go out, the party is over, and that chasm of emptiness engulfs their entire existence. The emptiness never really goes away; the drugs and alcohol just numb the pain of reality. In reality, life without God is lonely; there is no joy. There is an empty space that only he can fill. *Thou wilt shew me the path of life; in thy presence is fulness of joy; at thy right hand there are pleasures evermore.* (Psalms 16:11) What this scripture is saying is that God will show you the path through life if you will just follow him, and when you are following him or are in his presence, you will find the fullness of joy.

The Bible says that Jesus sits at the right hand of the Father. When we come to the Father's right hand, and we do that by coming through Jesus Christ, we will find pleasure evermore. The closest one will ever come to having no hassle, no worry, and unspeakable joy is to come to the Father through faith in his son Jesus. If you fully trust him and give your heart to him, then and only then can you have peace and contentment in your life. You will then know, whatever comes your way, whatever problems you may face, the Lord is with you and you can be strengthened by it. *We know that all things work together for good to them that love God.* (Rom. 8:28)

Our problem always goes back to a lack of trust in Jesus and unbelief in God. We hate to admit it but it is true. Jesus said, "Take up your cross and follow me," (Mark 8:34) but we want to follow the crowd. We want to be where it is happening. It is the in-thing to do. We justify ourselves by saying, "Everybody else is doing it. We won't be cool if we don't go along." God said, "*Obey my voice*," but we are afraid people will make fun of us. Kids say that parents just do not understand, and many times they do not because some are still making the same excuses for their own behavior.

Yes, I know all the excuses well; I have used them all at one time or another. I also know the feeling of looking over the fence at what I thought were greener pastures, and feeling as though the world was passing me by, being an outsider, envious of others. Someone once said, "When you feel yourself turning green with envy, you're ripe for trouble."

Looking back on it all, I guess I was fortunate to be broke. I will bet you are thinking, "That is an odd thing to say." I have never been really in need, but there never seemed to be any extra money floating around. Things were always pretty tight around our farm. I never considered us to be poor, though in some people's eyes I suppose we were. After all, my parents did not have a color television set until 1995, and to hear some people tell it, that is poverty.

No, I never considered us to be in poverty; that would be an awful situation to find yourself in. That would be shameful! That would be a disgrace, almost sinful! No, we were just broke.

I felt that I was in a really tough situation in high school. All the other kids would go out Friday and Saturday nights and spend Sunday afternoons riding around. We only had one family ride, a 1969 Chevrolet pickup, so I only got it on Saturday night. It was in the 1970's! The movie "Urban Cowboy" did not come out until 1980 so that was a time when driving a pickup definitely was not cool. Girls told me that they would not go out with a guy in a pickup. Boy, a statement like that will sure let the air out of a young man's party balloon. I mean, when you are a shy, broke teenager, it takes three months just to get up enough courage to ask a girl out; and if they said, "No," you could add another month to the three before the next attempt was made. All of this took place before the fool's hill episode, briefly mentioned earlier. During this period of my life, it seemed as though I was merely standing beside the road watching the world go by thinking with amazement just two things, "What a ride!" and "How can I get on?"

My cousin Tim, whom I mentioned earlier, finally found a niche that made him somewhat popular over night. He started playing the drums for a local band. All girls loved the band members even if they were broke. I kept telling him that he had it made; he had a reputation; he was in. He never did really understand the concept, and before long he had a steady and was talking about marriage.

I never could find my niche. When you were broke, that was strike one. When you drove a pick-up (back in those days), that was strike two. When you were a hog farmer, that was strike three, and it seemed as if no one understood. It was then that I met a true friend, one who could really understand the problems I faced. His name was Albert. He was broke; he drove a pickup; and he was a hog farmer. We used to sit in the Piggly Wiggly parking lot or at the Bay station in Abbeville, Al., while all the other kids drove up and down the road. We did not have the money for gas, and we could sit right there and see everybody in town. Occasionally someone would stop by and talk a few minutes, but for the most part, we just sat and talked about how broke we were. Now you are probably wondering what in the world has all this got to do with the statement that I made earlier about being fortunate to be broke. You see, if we had plenty of money we would, no doubt, have gotten into trouble. Instead, we sat and pondered the problems of the world. We discovered many truths during those conversations. We covered everything from politics to farm policy. I remember it distinctly, those words of wisdom, as Albert turned to me and said, "You know, if we were rich, Webster would have to redefine the word *fool,* because the definition he has now just wouldn't cover it." So, as you can see, I guess I was fortunate to be broke. I am sure it prevented a lot of heartache for my parents. Even though I was not squandering my possessions, through my thoughts and desires I was losing my substance because my thoughts and decisions were not a manifestation of God the Father. That was just the beginning. If one's thoughts and desires are headed in a certain direction, the body will soon follow, but a sin is committed already. Jesus gave an example of this in Matthew 5:28 when he said, "*Anyone who looks at a woman lustfully has already committed adultery with her in his heart*".

The prodigal son's sin started before he left home. It started in his mind, with his thoughts. His sinful thoughts turned to sinful decisions, and his sinful decisions turned to sinful actions. It did not take long for the thoughts to become actions. Where your mind goes your body will follow! Remember the shy fellow with the deflated party balloon who was so afraid of rejection? By the late 70's and early 80's the body was following the rebellious – no care attitude. He was totally different. So now when a young lady would make a snide remark like, "What can you do in a pickup truck," He would lean in close and whisper, "Baby we can do anything you want"! The sad thing is that many of the ladies liked that attitude so the acceptance caused him to sink deeper into depravity.

The Bible tells us that when the father divided his living between his sons that the younger son left not many days after. That is why we are told in Philippians 4:8 to think on the things that are true, honest, just, pure, lovely, and of good report. Our bodies will follow where our mind goes. What are you running through your mind these days? Are you spending enough time in the word of God? Are you spending enough time with him personally in prayer? If not, you may find yourself in a far-off country, a chasm of empty expanse, alone, without God; and you will wonder how you got there. It all starts with a thought. Think on the good things, the things of God. It will make a difference!

Chapter 3

LUKE 15: 14-15 BUT WHEN HE HAD SPENT ALL, THERE AROSE A SEVERE FAMINE IN THAT LAND, AND HE BEGAN TO BE IN WANT. THEN HE WENT AND JOINED HIMSELF TO A CITIZEN OF THAT COUNTRY, AND HE SENT HIM INTO HIS FIELDS TO FEED SWINE.

The Bible tells us that the young son began to be in want. What this means is that he began to be in physical want or need. His emotional wants or desires started back at home, and because those wants were not in line with the plan of the father, the son now found himself in physical need. The son loved power, money, wealth, and all that it could offer; but all of these things had let him down. In Matthew 5:24, Jesus told us that you cannot serve God and money. The son had shown by his ways that his master was money. Bad mistake! Jesus tells us in Matthew 6:25-34 that if we are in the Father's will, we will not have to worry because God will provide for our physical needs. Verse 33 says, "*Seek first the kingdom of God and his righteousness, and all these things shall be added to you.*" This son was seeking everything except righteousness, so he joined himself to a citizen of that country.

The citizen of this far-off country represents worldly people, people who do not know God, in a civilization contrary to God. To the Jewish people, God's chosen people, swine or pigs were considered unclean. During the Old Testament times, God's people were forbidden to use them for food. *Also the swine is unclean for you, because it has cloven hooves, yet does not chew the cud; you shall not eat their flesh or touch their dead carcasses. (Deut. 14:8)* God changes these rules in Acts, chapter 10, as a sign to the apostle Peter that salvation is not for Jews alone. During the time that this parable was told, the fact that this son had taken a job feeding swine was another sign of how far he had fallen in sin. (I have felt at times in my life that some still see feeding swine or raising hogs as sinful.)

Jesus did not tell us of the son's individual sins but about his lifestyle of sin. We humans try to categorize sin; by doing so, we attempt to justify our actions, saying our sin is not as bad as the sins of others. For example: I have heard many people quote scripture that says, in paraphrase, that homosexuality is an abomination to God, while they are having a sexual relationship outside of marriage. It is amazing how 1 Corinthians 6:9 is never mentioned. Those people should really check that one out. It puts fornicators—those who are having sexual relations outside of marriage—idolaters, adulterers, sodomites, thieves, drunkards, revelers, extortioners, and even those who covet, all in the same class. The Bible says they will not inherit the kingdom of heaven. Sin is sin in the eyes of God, and it only takes one sin to separate us from God. The Bible says in Rom. 6:23, that *"the wages of sin is death."* Notice the word *sin* does not have an *s* on the end of it. Death is the penalty for sin, not two sins or three sins, but one sin. When you see the word *death* in scripture, it means separation from God, and that is hell. God is a holy God, and he demands that his people be holy. The Bible tells us that "*...all have sinned and fall short of the glory of God.*" (Rom. 3:23) The only way we can be holy is on God's terms, and that is by a relationship through faith in his son, Jesus Christ. Do you have that relationship with Jesus? Are you living for Jesus, who died for you and rose again, as 2 Cor. 5:15 tells us we should? If you are not sure, give yourself a little test. Do you categorize sin, compare your sins to the sins of others, and try to convince yourself that your sins are not as bad as the sins of others? If you are trying to convince yourself that you do not, then you are guilty. Do you wonder how much sin you can commit and still make it to heaven? You're not even in the ballgame! As a matter of fact, you're not even in the town where the ball game is being played! If you were anywhere in the neighborhood you would be saying, "How far away from sin can I stay"?

I am not looking down my nose at you or pointing a finger to reveal your faults. I know how this works because, unfortunately, I have been there. My family and I have been hurt by people who claim to be Christians and claim to know Jesus. I remember saying, "If that person is going to heaven, then I know I'll get there." It sounds good, but there are major problems with a statement like that. First of all, mouth-action does not a Christian make. The gospels of Matthew and Luke record Jesus as he said, "A tree is known by his fruit." If the person is a spiritual person, he or she will bear spiritual fruit. *The fruit of the spirit is love, joy, peace, longsuffering, kindness, goodness, faithfulness, gentleness, self-control.* (Gal. 5:22-23) This means by one's actions and lifestyle you can know where they stand. There may be times when you are comparing yourself to a lost person, a person who knows as much about Jesus as the hogs that this young son was feeding. There are also those who, although they are Christians, have not grown in their relationship with Christ and are not being lead by the spirit. They may be children of God but not sons of God; there is a difference. Children of God are saved but have very little spiritual growth. Sons of God are lead by the spirit and, therefore, speak and act with the authority of God.

Another little test question is with whom do you associate? Who are your friends? With whom do you spend most of your time? Are you joined up with people who have a relationship with Christ, those who are living for Jesus, or are most of your friends living a life that is contrary to God? Do you use the scriptures to prove your point? Do you carefully pick out scriptures to justify your lifestyle, or do you read the Bible in search of what God has to say to you, even if it means you must admit you are wrong?

The Bible tells us that the son joined with a citizen of a far-off country. He was now getting what he desired all along, but things did not look quite as appealing from where he stood now as they did from the other side of the fence. He yearned for a life away from the father's discipline, and now he had it. He could not feel his father's discipline, but he could also not feel his father's love. He was now joined up with the world. The Bible is specific in telling us that we are not to love the world. *Love not the world, neither the things that are in the world. If any man love the world, the love of the father is not in him.* (1 John 2:15) John continues to say in the next verse that lust and pride are not of the Father, and these are the sins that have brought him to this place. He had a lust for freedom, but because of it he is now bound by sin. He had so much pride that he could not stand to be rejected by the world, so he rejected his father's love; and he later found out that the world had no love to offer. It was a sad situation and it got worse.

When we study these verses of scripture, we can see, without a doubt, there is no scientific evidence for evolution, because humans have not changed one bit in the last several thousand years. We still have that sinful nature that draws us to the world just like a moth being drawn to a flame, and the results are the same. Our only hope is that the wind of the Holy Spirit will blow us off our course of destruction.

The son had a desire to join up with the world, and where there is a will there is a way.

I also found that to be true in my life. I once thought that it was impossible to join up with the world; I thought that I was limited by my finances, by the vehicle I drove, or by my occupation. In my pursuit of acceptance, I found out that it was not about money, prestige, or my way of making a living. It was my attitude and my actions that made all the difference. For some strange reason, which I have yet to understand, the way to get worldly people's attention is to not care, just act if you do not care about your reputation, yourself, or the lives or feelings of others. People will say, "Man, he's cool. He don't care bout nothin." If those who are in the world think they cannot have your attention or affection and feel it is unattainable, they will try all the harder to get it. It seems to be the driving force behind them.

The problem with people in the world is not that they do not care, it is that they do not want to care. When you care about someone, you are vulnerable; you can be hurt easily. Humans will let you down. People do not want to be hurt, so they desire to be like the people who, they think, do not care about anyone or anything. I, like many in the world, learned to play the game. It is all really about deception. You hide the way you truly feel, and you pretend to be someone else. I wore a bright red and blue baseball cap with my new motto printed on it, "Who gives a s _ _ t! " You can fill in the blanks. I will give you a hint; it is the same thing as dung. If the people in the world cannot see the real you, the person who really does care, then you can remain in control. I think that is why the slogan for the antiperspirant commercial was so well remembered; you know the one, "Never let them see you sweat." You certainly do not want people to know that you are nervous, that you are not this unconcerned, cool person that you pretend to be. Like any other lie, you always have to be careful that no one finds out the truth.

It is always good to have a sidekick, a buddy to help you out of a tight situation. If someone is getting too close and is about to find out your secret that you are lonely; and you have an empty feeling in your soul the size of Texas, you need a diversion. My buddy Albert and I were in a nightclub one night talking with some young ladies. When things were about to get out of hand, it seemed as if they sensed that it was all an act. Albert pointed to me and asked the lady, "Do you see any concern in that eye or give a s _ _t in the other?" That was our line to throw people off track if they got too close. The lady, I think her name was Daphne, looked me straight in the eyes, paused, and said, "Yes, I do." The covers of my soul were pulled back, and she saw right into my heart. My buddy tried to cover quickly with another line, but it was too late. She knew. Though I felt a little embarrassed, there was also a warm feeling that someone understood. God used her, probably without her knowledge, to prick my heart and remind me that the person I was pretending to be was not really me. You can fool a lot of people, but you cannot fool God. God sees the emptiness and the hurt in your heart. All through this time in my life, he would put people who could see the truth in my path. I imagine they could see through my act because they were so much like me, hiding their true feelings and trying to be accepted by the world. It took a lot more pricks from the Lord to get me to turn from this lifestyle. I never saw the lady again, and she may never know that she was a dot on God's road map to lead me back to him. I hope God put someone in the paths of those whom he put in my path, so that they, too, could give up that lying lifestyle and turn back to him. That is what God desires—to let him fill that empty hole in your soul and give you a life worth living, full of joy, hope, and peace, with nothing to hide. What are you waiting for?

Chapter 4

LUKE 15:16 AND HE WOULD GLADLY HAVE FILLED HIS STOMACH WITH THE PODS THAT THE SWINE ATE, AND NO ONE GAVE HIM ANYTHING.

There used to be a commercial on television promoting a drug free lifestyle. The commercial showed a lot of kids telling what they wanted to be when they grew up. The next scene was of a guy dressed in a coat and tie crawling around on the floor of a resort stall picking up some drugs that he had dropped, as the announcer said, "Nobody ever says they want to be a junkie when they grow up."

That commercial would have really hit home to this young Jewish boy. Never, in his wildest dreams, would he have believed that he could have stooped so low. His lifestyle of wallowing in sin had him now wallowing with the hogs, but at this point he was just like the junkie. He did not even realize he had a problem.

Swine were unclean to Jewish people and they had no use for them. Because they had no use for the hogs, they also had no use for the people who raised them. [I think I have run across some people in my life who have a dominant Jewish gene, because they seem to have the same attitude toward people who raise hogs today.] Yet, here was a young Jewish boy, who not only was associating with people who raised hogs, but he gladly ate with the hogs.

Down South we would say, "He dun gone back on his raisin.'" The English translation of that is that the way he was acting was not the way he was reared or taught to act.

When we see someone acting in a way that is contrary to the way we know they have been taught, we often ask, " Why are they acting in such a rebellious manner?" To answer this question, we must first remember what has brought them to this place. Most times it is worldly lust and a desire to be accepted. People want to be looked up to; they want to feel important.

The Jewish boy, we will call him Fred since we are not told his name, did still not realize he had a problem because Fred was comparing himself to people of the world. The hogs in this parable represent Satan's children. The devil has children, those who live a life contrary to God and are not concerned with spiritual matters or God's desire for their lives. Jesus told a group in John 8:44, "*You are of your father the devil.*" The hogs wallowing in the mud are like worldly people wallowing in sin; they like it. They have no room for God in their lives. The Bible tells us more about them. *The fool hath said in his heart, there is no God.* (Psalms 14:1) The original text says a fool hath said in his heart that there is no God. This could be read as saying even a fool knows there is a God. He just has no interest or desire for God. I will give you an example. Let us say that you have just finished a big meal. Your host (my mother-in-law) comes to you holding one of her famous strawberry pies. With one hand on your stomach, you wave with the other and say, "No pie." What you are saying is not that you do not believe there is pie, but just no pie for you. You are not interested in strawberry pie or have no desire for strawberry pie. To have no desire for my mother-in-law's strawberry pie, one must be mentally impaired. The Bible says that to have no desire for or no interest in God is a foolish thing; yet many foolish people are hiding behind PhD's. They flaunt their worldly intelligence with a holier-than-thou attitude when they have no ability whatsoever to discern spiritual matters. They can explain the laws of physics, yet the Bible seems foolish to them. The scriptures explain this phenomenon in the second chapter of 1 Corinthians. *The natural man does not receive the things of the spirit of God, for they are foolishness to him; nor can he know them, because they are spiritually discerned.* (1Cor. 2:14) When they read the word of God, they laugh and call it foolishness. God's word has something to say about that, too! *The foolishness of God is wiser than man's wisdom.* (1 Cor. 1:25)

Fred, so blinded by the desire to be accepted and admired, now found himself in the hog pen. He did not realize the seriousness of his condition because he was surrounded by those who looked up to him. They made him feel appreciated when he came carrying the feed bucket. They squealed with joy when they saw him. It may sound silly, but remember, the hogs represent the worldly people, and their actions have a lot of similarities. You see, people of the world are only interested in helping themselves. Their number one thought is what they are going to get out of the deal. They will give you respect only if they get something in return. They will look up to you and sing your praises as long as you keep providing them with a free lunch.

If you have no desire for God, if you are really enjoying your sinful lifestyle, if there is not heaviness in your heart about it, then you do not belong to God. You are not his child, and that is a dangerous place to be. I hope you do not breathe your last breath in that condition. When a sinner dies in his sin, he is no better than a dead hog in the feedlot. When a hog dies, his owner gives him over to the pit or the incinerator. When a person dies without Christ, God gives them over to the pit as well. It is a tragedy for the hog farmer because he loses money on a lost animal. It is a tragedy when a person dies and goes to the pit after God has given his only begotten son to pay the price for their sin. Where do you stand?

The Bible said that Fred would have gladly filled his stomach with the husk that the hogs ate. The word *gladly* is translated *fain* in the King James Version. The actual Greek word here is *epithumeo*, pronounced *ep-ee-thoo-meh'-o*. It means to set the heart upon, long for, covet, desire, or lust after. It was his desires and lust that had brought him to this point in his life; it was his desires and lust that he had turned to the world to satisfy; and yet the desires and lust were still eating away at his very being. He still had not realized that those lust and desires could not be satisfied.

People today are struggling to fulfill those same lust and desires. We call it working for a living. We say we can barely make it working seven days a week. We spend all those extra hours in overtime, while many times neglecting our family's problems and heartaches. We miss those special times of watching our children grow up. We miss too many little league ball games or music recitals in search of the almighty dollar, all the while claiming we are doing it for our families. We say we want them to have a better life, while rejecting the most important things we can give to our family and that is time and love. One day the money will be spent, the new cars will be rusted out, and our families will be left with nothing but the lust and desire to get more stuff. Your lifestyle may be fueling the fires of lust and desire in the family that God has entrusted to your care. These worldly lusts and desires can never be satisfied, but they can be removed. They can only be replaced with love for God. If you truly love the Lord, then your desire becomes serving him and doing his will. If you continue spiritually in the world, then your fear of being accepted will never be completely overcome. *The fear of the wicked will come upon him. The desire of the righteous will be granted.* (Prov. 10:24) It is not by our own goodness or works that we are made righteous, but our faith in Jesus and his sacrifice on Calvary that makes us righteous. *Not having my own righteousness, which is from the law, but that which is through faith in Christ, the righteousness which is from God by faith.* (Phil. 3:9) When you receive the righteousness from God through your faith in Christ, God will begin to remove envy and earthly desires from your heart. The only things you should covet are the gifts God offers. *But covet earnestly the best gifts.* (1 Cor. 12:31) At this point, the only thing Fred was coveting was something to fill his belly, but what he had not realized was that when a child of God fills his belly with the things that the world feeds upon, the child of God will still not be satisfied.

Young son Fred was now showing signs of conviction, but instead of giving in and asking forgiveness, he was still comparing himself to Satan's children. Now, instead of having them look up to him, he was now face to face with them. If you are going to eat with the pigs, you have to get on the same level with them. He started trying to convince himself that he was really in pretty good company. After all, those pigs were in good shape; they did not have to take on any responsibility; their needs were being met; and they seemed to be happy. Fred said, " Don't worry about me, folks. I'm doing fine down here in this hog parlor." Since the world has become so scientifically and technologically advanced, we now have hog parlors instead of hog pens. It sounds a lot better, but the same thing that is lying on the ground in the hog pen is also lying on the floor of the hog parlor, and *it* is just like sin. If you are not looking you will step right in *it*, and when *it* gets on you everyone will know it, even if they do not mention *it*. To some, *it* and sin are repulsive, and they will hold their noses, or turn them up, according to whether it is sin or *it* that you are talking about. With either one, this group will keep their distance from you. These are like the Pharisees mentioned in the Bible. The Pharisees paraded around with long robes with their noses held so high they did not notice what their garments were dragging through. On the other hand, you have those who never mention anything to you because they are used to the odor, whether the odor comes from sin or *it*. *It* and sin are really very much alike. If you stay around them both for a long time, they do not bother you as much, but with sin that can be very dangerous. Those who are not bothered by sin are lost. They have surrounded themselves so much by sin that it has become their way of life. There is another group who recognize the odor, whether it is from sin or *it*. They do not look down on you, and they do not want to hurt you; they truly care about you. They gently try to point the way to correct the problem, even lend a hand if the need arises. These are the ones who are led by God, the sons and daughters of God, the true Christians. These are the people you expect to find in our churches today. Unfortunately, you will find the Pharisee group there, too. That is why many people remain in the hog pen. They had rather surround themselves with people who will not mention their problem than be ridiculed by someone with *it* on the tails of their long robes.

A group of pastors and I were serving at a weekend spiritual event. We had all given talks, shared our mistakes and failures, as well as giving glory to God for getting us back on the right track. A gentleman that was there asked if he could speak to the group of pastors. Of course we obliged. He said, "You have no idea how much power and encouragement it gives us when you leave your cloaks at the door and act like normal guys"! We responded, "We don't have a cloak and we are normal guys!" We are all human and we all make mistakes. The Bible tells us in Romans 12:3 not to think of oneself more highly than he ought and Galatians 6:1 tells us that *if a man is overtaken in any trespass, you who are spiritual restore such a one in the spirit of gentleness, considering yourself, lest you also be tempted.* We must be ever mindful of the Spirit as we bring correction to others.

So, here we have Fred, still in the hog pen; but what Fred seems to have forgotten was that those pigs were going to slaughter, and they would be separated from all the good things that they now enjoyed, just as Satan's children are going to be eternally separated from all the good things they now have because they will be eternally separated from God. The Bible tells us that all good things come from God. *Charge them that are rich in this world, that they be not highminded, nor trust in uncertain riches, but in the living God, who giveth us richly all things to enjoy.* (1 Timothy 6:17) Unfortunately, many people refuse to thank God and give him the glory for all the good things they have. Have you thanked God for the good things in your life today?

When some find themselves in the hog pen of life, nothing is going right. Murphy's Law (if anything can go wrong, it will) seems to be ruling their life; they blame God. Blinded by pride, they cry out, " If there really is a God, you would not let this awful thing happen to me." Pride is like insulin. Our body needs a small amount of it, but too much can be deadly. Pride comes from spending too much time exalting self. We should spend more time exalting others. *Whoever exalts himself will be humbled, and he who humbles himself will be exalted.* (Mat. 23:12) To humble ourselves before God means to come respectfully before him, understanding that we are totally dependent upon him. When we do this, confessing our sin, the Bible says in 1 John 1:9 that he is faithful and just to forgive our sin, and to cleanse us from all unrighteousness. *If we say that we have no sin, we deceive ourselves, and the truth is not in us.* (1John 1:8)

Are you still in the hog pen wallowing in sin? Are you still comparing yourself to the hogs, trying to convince yourself that everything is all right? Whatever you do, do not let pride keep you from a relationship with the Lord. *A man's pride will bring him low, but the humble in spirit will retain honor.* (Prov. 29:23)

Chapter 5

LUKE 15:17 BUT WHEN HE CAME TO HIMSELF, HE SAID, "HOW MANY OF MY FATHER'S HIRED SERVANTS HAVE BREAD ENOUGH AND TO SPARE, AND I PERISH WITH HUNGER!"

In earlier chapters, we mentioned that this young son represented one of God's children who had strayed away from his father's will. We only say this because we know the rest of the story. It would be more scripturally correct to say, he was a child that God was dealing with. The scriptural correctness of this statement will be covered later. If we only looked at what we had read so far, we would think he is just a hellion that ain't worth the salt that goes in his bread, as we would say in the south. In other words, you would question his ability to even be saved. In his ability it is impossible, *but with God all things are possible.* (Mat. 19:26) He was living in a manner that was totally against his nature. Many times people judge others by their actions, although their actions may not always align with their hearts. Even though it was his lust and desires that caused his problems, the Holy Spirit, whether abiding in his heart, or leaning over his shoulder whispering in his spiritual ear was convicting him of his actions. With the scripture we have read so far, we can only speculate. Later we will discover the Holy Spirit was leaning over his shoulder and whispering in his ear not abiding within him. I know that will go against some of your belief, but just hang on! I am not claiming to have some special revelation. God's Word tells us but we haven't gotten to that yet. We will discuss that later!

The Holy Spirit will never let one of God's children feel comfortable in a life of sin, and will also bring conviction on those who are not His children, so they too will have the opportunity to become His sons and daughters. Conviction is one of the spirit's many jobs. Jesus, speaking of the Holy Spirit, said, "*When he has come, he will convict the world of sin.*" (John 16:8)

One might wonder how a young Jewish boy who we earlier named Fred, raised in the instruction of God's Word, could find himself in such a situation. The problem was his youth, not his age but his spiritual immaturity. In order to fight off the snares of the world, we must grow spiritually. Just as a baby would not stand a chance of survival if placed out in the wilderness, an immature Christian will not stand a chance against the wilds of the world. Second Peter 3:18 says that we should grow in grace and knowledge of our Lord and Savior, Jesus Christ. When we grow in knowledge of Christ, we grow in knowledge of God. Jesus said in John 14:9, "*He who has seen me has seen the Father*". Jesus has the full authority of God the Father.

Often in scripture we see references to children of God and sons of God. There is a difference! A child of God believes in God and has accepted the provision that God has made for their salvation. That provision is the payment for our sin made by the death of his sinless son, Jesus Christ, on the cross at Calvary and by his resurrection and ascension to the right hand of the father. This we accept by faith. Through this faith we become children of God. Romans 8:14 tells us that to be sons of God, you are to be led by the spirit of God. *For as many as are led by the spirit of God, these are the sons of God.* (Rom. 8:14) The words translated from the Greek text for *child* and *son* are not always interchangeable. You may be a child of God and not a son of God, but you must be child of God in order to become a son of God. Say what?

I will try to explain what I mean without confusing you any further. In verse 5 of Ephesians chapter one, we find that God says, "*He has predestined us to adoption as sons by Jesus Christ to himself.*" In our western culture we adopt children who are biologically not our own; however, in eastern culture they adopt their own children. Say what? As an example, let us say that a man owns a business, and he has a little boy. The father provides the finest education possible for his child. He is taught all the basic necessities to function in the business world. He is then taught specifically about the father's business. Not only is he taught about the business itself, but he is taught the father's vision for the future of the business. The father's vision becomes the son's vision. When the son has matured to the point that they share the same vision, there is a big celebration. The father's son stands in front of the crowd and the father says, "This is my beloved son of whom I am well pleased." Do those words sound familiar? They are the same words God spoke from heaven at the baptism of Jesus. Jesus was always God's son, but God was announcing to the world that Jesus had his authority; he had his vision. The words he spoke would be God's words; the deeds he did would be God's deeds. God was saying that everything Jesus did would be in direct correlation with his plan. That is why Jesus said, "When you have seen me, you have seen the Father." Jesus was saying that every thing he did, everything he said, and every move he made was exactly the way God the Father wanted it done. He had the authority to act on behalf of God the Father. You see, to be a son of God, one is to have the authority of God. He should be a mature Christian who desires to do the will of the Father. His decisions should be based on the desire of the Father, which will be made known through the Holy Spirit. That is why sons of God are to be led by the spirit of God.

Young son Fred was not mature enough to face the wilds of the world on his own. I will tell you a little secret; he never would be mature enough on his own. One can only face the wilds of this world through the power of the Holy Spirit, because it is through the power of the Holy Spirit that we receive divine guidance from God. The majority of humans' problems stem from the fact that we are trying to beat our way through this worldly wilderness on our own, and we become weary and worn. It is then that we become vulnerable to the attacks of Satan. He tantalizes us with visions of our desires, but they are only a mirage. He lures us with our own worldly lusts and passions. He holds us, not with life, but with an illusion of life.

While we are wading through the dung in the pigpen of life, Satan convinces us we are in a palace. If we would but listen to God and heed the conviction of the Holy Spirit, God would lift us out of the dunghill we are in. *He hath raised up the poor out of the dust, and lifted the needy out of the dunghill.* (Ps. 113:7) If we would but surrender our hearts and lives totally to God, he would replace those worldly lusts with a passion for witnessing and replace our desires with his desires.

Many professing Christians never fully submit their hearts and lives totally to Christ. Their faith is nothing more than a bogus fire insurance policy. They are not really looking forward to heaven, but they have heard enough about hell that they are sure they do not want to go to there. The problem with this kind of faith is that it is not really faith at all. They have knowledge of God in their head but nothing in their heart. They believe as long as they do not have to change their lifestyle. All demons believe in God, but they will spend eternity in hell. *You believe there is one God. You do well. Even the demons believe and tremble.* (James 2:19) All demons believe that Jesus is the Son of God, but they refuse to follow him. Luke tells us in chapter 8 of his gospel about a man possessed by demons. *When he saw Jesus, he cried out, and fell down before him, and with a loud voice said, "What have I to do with thee, Jesus, thou son of God most high*?" (Luke 8:28) The demons recognized Jesus as the Son of God; they refused to follow him, but even they must respect his authority. Some may think they can snub their nose at Jesus, but there will come a day when every knee will bow and acknowledge that Jesus Christ is Lord. *Therefore God also has highly exalted him and given him the name which is above every name, that at the name of Jesus every knee should bow, of those in heaven, and of those on earth, and of those under the earth, and that every tongue should confess that Jesus Christ is Lord, to the glory of God the father.* (Philippians 2: 9-11) Submit now or submit later; either way, one day you will submit to the authority of Jesus Christ. Submit now unto his leadership and guidance, or submit later to his judgment. *For the father judges no one, but has committed all judgment to the son.* (John 5: 22) Submission, now or later; which will it be?

The Bible says that the young son came to himself. Sometimes it takes the jolt of hitting rock bottom to wake us up. We realize that we are different from the hogs. Surely we may be eating with the hogs, we may be as filthy as the hogs, and we may even smell like the hogs, but there is one huge difference. We do not really enjoy wallowing in the mud like the hogs; we do not really enjoy that sinful lifestyle. We have convinced others that we like it; we may have almost convinced ourselves, but the Holy Spirit will always remind us of who we really are or who we should be. The most miserable person on the face of the earth is not the drug addict, alcoholic, thief, prostitute, fornicator, or murderer. It is the child of God who is living in disobedience, outside the will of God! When people say they were saved as a little child and wandered away from God for twenty or thirty years and then came back to the Lord; I say, "There is a Greek word for that". Baloney!!! You might say, "You don't believe people can do that preacher?" Extremely unlikely! It is not that it is impossible because with God all things are possible but I'm sure it happens less often than people are led to believe. Many, who think they have been saved, have really only had an experience with God. There is more conviction on a saved person who has truly experienced the saving grace of the Lord Jesus Christ than there is on the lost person. Once you have known the peace that Christ gives, I cannot imagine someone being able live for years without it. The conviction, the fear, the doubt, the alone feeling is tormenting. You long and yearn for the peace and contentment you had in the presence of the Lord. I experienced 20 years outside God's will one week! That week seemed like 20 years! I spent a week trying to figure out what was wrong. Then I prayed and asked God what was wrong. He spoke to me and revealed to me my sin. I repented and begged Him to give me another chance! He did! I should have asked Him first instead of trying to figure it out myself! Lesson learned!

If you are not a true child of God, the spirit will be working on the outside of you, trying to guide you out of the mire and the muck to a better life, a contented life, and certainly a cleaner life. If you continue to resist the conviction of the Holy Spirit, your conscience will become seared; it will be rendered insensitive. The Bible tells us this reaction will be more prevalent in the last days. *Now the spirit expressly says that in latter times some will depart from the faith, giving heed to deceiving spirits and doctrines of demons, speaking lies in hypocrisy, having their own conscience seared with a hot iron.* (1Timothy 4:1-2) This is taking place all around you as you read these words. It does not happen fast. It is a slow process; our senses are dulled to what is right and wrong because of the constant bombardment of ungodliness, which seems to become more accepted as each day passes. We are in the last days!

When you have not followed God but have followed your lusts and desires for so long, it is sometimes hard to know whether the spirit is working from the inside or the outside. You may not be sure of your salvation, and you may even question others when they say that they are sure of theirs. You have put your trust in people so many times and they have let you down, so you are not sure you can trust God's plan for your salvation. You may feel like nobody loves you, so why would God be concerned? Believe me. He is! You may be thinking that God could not possibly love you; you think you are not good enough. God's love has nothing to do with whether you are good or bad. God just loves you! *God demonstrates his own love toward us, in that while we were still sinners, Christ died for us.* (Rom. 5:8) The young man came to himself; he could no longer resist the conviction of the Holy Spirit. He had reached a position of humiliation and disgust.

Some biblical scholars may question me on the previous statement. They may say that the Bible does not tell us his feelings and that I cannot know for sure what he felt. I can and I do because I have been there. I have experienced all his fears, all his desires, his lusts, his emptiness, his failures, his humiliation, and his disgust.

I walked the aisle and joined the church at the age of twelve. I knew I was a sinner. I needed Jesus in my life, but I also had a desire to be accepted by my peers. I did not understand that God could grant me the power through the Holy Spirit to overcome the pressures of life. I was taught of faith and belief, but I knew nothing of being spirit-led or being filled with the power available through the Holy Spirit. I was trying to live my life through my own human ability, and I failed miserably. I would be elbow-deep in sin, walking through the pigpen of life all during the week and be sitting in church on Sunday morning acting like everything was wonderful. As I grew older, I played the games of deceit during the week, pretending to be the cool cowboy at the honky- tonks on Friday night and playing church on Sunday, teaching a youth Sunday school class. I tried to keep my reputation clean with the church folks by frequenting different clubs than they did. Yes, you read that right; when I saw a fine, upstanding church member coming out of a bar, it made it a lot easier to justify my actions. The Bible says we should be careful not to be a stumbling block for other Christians. *It is good neither to eat meat nor drink wine nor do anything by which your brother stumbles or is offended or is made weak.* (Rom. 14:21) I was trying to keep one foot in the world and one foot in the church. I wanted to have my cake and eat it too. You might say, I was straddling the fence. I was staying in the middle of the road, and I personally could not see any difference between the majority of the church members that I knew and myself. There were a few who seemed different, but I felt I could never measure up to their standards. I knew I had sinned, and there were certain people who would constantly remind me of my imperfections, so I began to classify different sins in an attempt to justify myself before God. For example: cursing would not be as bad as fornication, which was not as bad as adultery, which was not as bad as not believing something in the Bible, which was not as bad as homosexuality. I would say to myself, "Surely, God, if you are going to let that person in heaven, I'll make it too." The problem with that line of thought is that many times I was comparing myself to other people in the hog pen or the hogs themselves. Yes, I know it sounds stupid, and it is; yet millions and millions of people are doing the same thing.

If only I could have had someone close to my age, one of those few who seemed so perfect, explain that I could stand perfect, blameless before God by believing that Jesus Christ had paid the penalty for my sin and totally submitting and following the lead of the Holy Spirit. If only I had known that they too would accept and forgive me as Jesus would, I just might not have stayed in the pigpen of sin so long. There were a few young ladies that I felt were the perfect Christian role models, but I was too shy and afraid to question them about my problem. I was in my mid-thirties before I found a man my age that I knew was truly sold out to God. He was a redneck to the core, and he did not deny it; but he was a blood-washed, spirit-filled, Jesus-following redneck. He did not seem to be as perfect as the ladies I knew. But then, I have always felt that the ladies were more perfect than men. If nothing else, they are certainly more pleasing to the eyes. The thing that was so prevalent in this man's life was his love of God and his desire to follow Christ. That is what made him different. Thank you, Andy Bryan, for being God's fire for me in a cold, cold world. You are a friend and an inspiration.

Many people in the churches today act as if rednecks cannot get into heaven. They look down on them because they feel they are ignorant and unlearned. It seems to me that the apostles would fit in this category very easily. *Now when they saw the boldness of Peter and John, and perceived that they were uneducated and untrained men, they marveled. And they realized that they had been with Jesus.* (Acts 4:13) I thank God that he looks at us differently than our fellow man does.

Education and training is a good thing, but sometimes it may get in the way of ministry. People may be intimidated, afraid to talk to you because of your "education". I prefer that people just recognize that I have been with Jesus! It seems that I'm able to reach more people if they don't know I have a title. Most religious people do not seem to understand the fact that being with Jesus and being led by the Spirit is more important than title, education, or training. Let's face facts; it's more impressive for a redneck to do something beyond his ability than a man with briefcase and a diploma. I don't know about other folk, but if I had not spent some time with Jesus, there would be no diploma. It was only my surrender to Christ and the hunger He gave me for his word that allowed me to accomplish anything. I don't care about how much someone thinks I know; I just want them to know and follow who I know and follow!

What a difference it would make in this world if those in the hog pen of life could see professing Christians following the teachings of Christ. Instead, they follow the teaching of the Pharisees; they are so afraid they will defile themselves that they never reach out to those in need. Christianity is not a *thou-shalt-not* religion; it is a *go-and-do* relationship with Christ. Jesus came to serve, to reach out to the lost, and he tells us to go and do likewise. Many who claim to know the Lord are like the priest and the Levite in the story of the Good Samaritan. They are not walking in the middle of the road, but they are on the wrong side.

Too many people are trying to stay in the middle of the road. My pastor of some thirty-plus years, Brother Ed Holloway, has an eloquent way of explaining the problem with this activity. He says, "There is nothing in the middle of the road but a yellow line and a dead possum." You will not enter heaven standing in the middle of the road. You have to be on the right or the left. Jesus basically said, "You are either for me or against me. There is no middle ground." Jesus told the church members at Laodicea that they were neither hot nor cold; they were lukewarm, and it made him sick to his stomach. *So then, because you are lukewarm, and neither cold nor hot, I will vomit you out of my mouth.* (Rev. 3:16) Being in a position which makes the King of kings and Lord of lords the one who will judge the world want to puke is not a smart place to be. I thank God that I came to myself! Are you still trying to walk in the middle of the road? Are you still straddling the fence? If you are not totally for Jesus, then you are against him. God wants all of you, and he will not take part of you. It is all or nothing. It is decision time. Which will it be?

Chapter 6

Luke 15: 18-19 I will arise and go to my father, and will say to him, "Father I have sinned against heaven and before you, and am no longer worthy to be called your son. Make me like one of your hired servants."

In the previous verses of Luke, chapter 15, we saw a son turn from his father's will and live a life of sin. Now we find him recognizing his fallen condition and making the decision to turn back to the father in humble repentance.

When someone truly turns to God in repentance, he does so with a humble attitude. He does not climb out of the hog lot, take a shower, wash his clothes, put on deodorant and cologne, then walk up to God and say, "I am being good now. What are you going to do for me?" Yet, that is the attitude some people have toward God. They complain about their life and say, "I've cleaned myself up. I've tried living right, and God has still let all these bad things happen to me." Their problem is that they cannot clean themselves up. Even on our best day we will still reek with the odor of sin. No matter how much we wash with soap and water, God can still see the stains of sin in our lives. There is only one thing that can cleanse us of those stains, and that is the precious blood of Jesus. God is a just and righteous God, and because He is just, He must bring justice to those who break the law. The Bible tells us that *the wages of sin is death.* (Rom. 6:23) Therefore the payment for sin requires death, and one can only be purified by blood. *According to the law almost all things are purified by blood, and without shedding of blood there is no remission.* (Heb. 9:22) Jesus Christ paid the price with His blood that we might go free! The words of that old hymn are so true:

> What can wash away my sin?
> Nothing but the blood of Jesus.
> What can make me whole again?
> Nothing but the blood of Jesus.
>
> Oh, precious is the flow,
> That makes me white as snow.
> No other fount I know,
> Nothing but the blood of Jesus.

I have heard many people say, "I'll come back to church when I get my life straightened out." The problem with that is they never will. They cannot, but God can! Come back to church, listen to the preaching and teaching of God's word, submit your life to God, spend some time in prayer, and let him straighten you out. The old hymn, one of my favorites, does not say, "All clean and bright I come to thee." It says:

> Just as I am, without one plea,
> But that Thy blood was shed for me,
> And that Thou bidd'st me come to Thee,
> O Lamb of God, I come! I come!

God is calling us; the Holy Spirit is convicting us; and we are to come without a plea, not declaring ourselves to be innocent, because we are not. We are guilty; we are sinners. *As it is written: there is none righteous, no, not one.* (Rom. 3:10)

> Just as I am, and waiting not,
> To rid my soul of one dark blot,
> To Thee whose blood can cleanse each spot,
> O Lamb of God, I come! I come!

We should not wait and try to clean ourselves up. We are to come as we are, and let Jesus do the cleaning. Just as the song says, he will never turn you away. He will receive you; and he will cleanse you if you will allow him, if you trust him, if you believe in him.

> Just as I am, Thou wilt receive,
> Wilt welcome, pardon, cleanse, relieve,
> Because Thy promise I believe,
> O Lamb of God, I come! I come!

Jesus will welcome you into the family of God, or welcome you home if you have strayed, like the young son. He will pardon you from the wages of sin, which is eternal separation from God. He will cleanse you from all unrighteousness, and he will relieve you from the guilt that you carry.

How do I know that he will do all these things? I know this because Jesus is no mortal man; He is the very word of God. He has given his word that he would do these things, and his very being is filled with grace and truth. *And the word became flesh and dwelt among us, and we beheld his glory, the glory as of the only begotten of the father, full of grace and truth.* (John 1:14) Another reason that I know Jesus will do these things is because he has done them for me.

Before Jesus will welcome, pardon, cleanse, and relieve, you must turn to him. In order to turn to Jesus, you must turn away from sin. Turn away from your lifestyle of sin and live your life for Christ. *Those who live should live no longer for themselves, but for him who died for them and rose again.* (2 Cor. 5:15) Jesus said, "*You must repent! But unless you repent you will all likewise perish.*" (Luke 13:5) The Greek word for repent here is *metanoeo*, pronounced *met-an-o-eh-o*. It means to think differently or reconsider. The young Jewish boy had no doubt begun to think differently. He had begun to reconsider his position in life, as even the life of his father's servants seemed much better than the life he had been living, and it was true. The hired servants had shelter and food, their needs were met, but he stood in the mud and slop, with no food nor shelter, in a world where no one cared enough to lend a helping hand.

No one cares in a world away from God, or if they do they will not show it because caring is a sign of weakness to people of the world. Worldly people laugh at you when you are hurting and will kick you while you are down. There have been times in my life that I have been kicked, and I am sorry to say there have been times that I have done the kicking. A hurting word, many times, is worse than a kick in the stomach. I know because I have felt those words from people in the world that I have looked up to, and I have seen the hurt on the face of those of whom I have hurt. Oh, what I would give to be able to undo the damage I have done to many people's lives, but for some, I cannot. There have been times I believe the things I said may have been the one thing that sent a person into a downward spiral, never to recover. I cannot help but believe that their destruction came from a hurting word or a shove in the wrong direction—a shove to the young fellow I met from Indiana who was killed in a car accident or a hurting word to the young lady who married the drug dealer and was murdered. Now all I can do is ask God for forgiveness. I have and he has, but I cannot help wondering what would have happened if I had been living for Jesus, "*him who died for me,*" instead of living for self. Where would they be and where would I be if I had only followed Christ instead of my selfish desires?

The young son was no longer looking for the power and prestige that he once desired and probably thought he deserved. He now saw himself for what we all are, sinners, in need of a Savior. He knew that without help he would always be in the pigpen of life, and he would always be in want. That empty feeling would never be filled in the world. His desires had now begun to change. Instead of wanting a life away from the father, his only desire was to serve him.

I am sure he remembered the life he had with the father, and I am sure they were fond memories. Oh, how he wished he could have that life back, but he knew he did not deserve it, and he would never ask for it. He only hoped that the father would allow him to be his servant. That is what humility is all about! Have you come to God desiring to be his servant, or are you coming desiring fire insurance? Do you only want just enough faith to keep you out of hell?

There will be some who will just barely make it to heaven, you might say, by the skin of their teeth, but some will go first class. There are those who claim to be doing the Lord's work that would not be doing it at all if it were not for the earthly fame or recognition they receive. Then there are those who just want to serve the Lord. Many times here on earth we may not know the difference, but the time will come when "*each one's work will become clear; for the day will declare it, because it will be revealed by fire; and the fire will test each one's work of what sort it is.*" (1 Cor. 3:13) In verse 14 of 1 Corinthians, chapter three, God's word tells us that when our works are tried by fire and endure we will receive a reward. What this means is that if these works are done in a humble spirit, not for fame or self-acclaim, but out of love for God, we will be rewarded. If they are done for earthly recognition, that will be all we will get, and worldly recognition will not last. The scripture goes on to say that *if anyone's work is burned, he will suffer loss; but he himself will be saved, yet so as through fire.* (1 Cor. 3:15) These are the ones who will make it to heaven by the skin of their teeth. They may be there, but they may have a smell of smoke about them. When you come to yourself and you are looking nose to nose with the hogs of the world, wallowing in the same mud hole and eating from the same trough, it is much easier to be humble.

There was always something that kept me a little uncomfortable with my past lifestyle of sin. I was a user, not of drugs, but of people. Though many around me thought it was cool, I could not help but notice the hurt on the faces of those who discovered they were being used. I knew the look, because I had been there myself, and I had no intention of going back. The only way I thought I could keep from being used was to be the user. Even though I had joined the church at the age of twelve, at that time in my life I was not sure where I would go when I died. I did not know for sure whether the Holy Spirit was working on the inside of me or from the outside, but I did know he was working, and looking back, I thank God he was working. My own actions became disgusting to me. I could not bear to see, in another person's eyes, the heartache that I was causing. My worldly lifestyle was making me sick to my stomach. I remember asking myself, "Why am I acting this way?"

To answer this question, I think we are bombarded with these worldly ideals constantly, even through the cartoons our children watch. I remember Garfield, after winning a talent contest said, "On the way up, I don't care whom I step on because I'm not coming back down." Although Garfield was brought back down to earth in the cartoon, that phrase sticks with people. In the eyes of God,

Garfield was actually not on his way up, but on his way down. God looks at things differently than we do, and as Christians we should look at things God's way. When considering how to handle a problem in life, it would be a sure bet that God's solution to the problem will be opposite from man's opinion.

For example, human nature says, "Stand tall;" God's word says, "*Humble yourself.*" *Whosoever therefore shall humble himself as this little child; the same is greatest in the kingdom of heaven.* (Mat. 18:4) Human nature says, "Be proud." God's word says, "W*hen pride cometh, then cometh shame.*" (Prov. 11:2) Human nature says, "Use people before they use you." God says, "*Love your neighbor as yourself.*" (Mat. 22:39) Human nature says, "Get revenge." God says, "*Do good to them that hate you.*" (Lk. 6:27) Human nature says, "Help only those who can help you in return." God says, "*Do good and lend, hoping for nothing in return; and your reward will be great.*" (Lk. 6:35) Why, you might ask, are the ideals of human nature so different from the ideals of God? It is because *the natural man receiveth not the things of the spirit of God: for they are foolishness unto him: neither can he know them, because they are spiritually discerned.*" (1 Cor. 2:14)

One must be led by the spirit in order to receive the things from God, because "*God has revealed them unto us by his spirit; for the spirit searches all things, yes, the deep things of God.*" (1 Cor 2:10) Are you being led by the spirit, or are you being led by the natural man within you? If you are not being led by the spirit, chances are, you are going against the will of God; you are carnal minded. *For to be carnally minded is death; but to be spiritually minded is life and peace.* (Rom. 8:6) The Bible goes on to say in verse 7, *the carnal mind is enmity against God.* In other words, the carnal mind is an enemy of God. What is a carnal mind? We think of it as being lewd or crude, but the Greek word here actually means your human nature; so when we make excuses for our actions by saying, "That's just being human," it is not a viable excuse. The human nature is an enemy of God. So who are you, friend or enemy? Not sure? Where is your mind? Is it on the carnal or on the spiritual? Are you headed for death or life and peace?

Chapter 7

LUKE 15:20 AND HE AROSE AND CAME TO HIS FATHER, BUT WHEN HE WAS STILL A GREAT WAY OFF, HIS FATHER SAW HIM AND HAD COMPASSION, AND RAN AND FELL ON HIS NECK AND KISSED HIM.

We see in this scripture that the son had changed his direction in life. Unfortunately, many of us have to be flat of our backs in the slop, in the pigpen of life, before we change our direction. We have our plan for our life, and because of our pride we stick to it, no matter how deep it takes us.

I had a plan for my life, but I realized a number of years ago that my plan was not going to work out. My father and I started farming jointly around 1977. 1980 was a disaster! We made 400 lbs. of peanuts to the acre that year and with input costs rising I figured it took about 2000 lbs. per acre to break even. Our corn only made 15 bushels to the acre and the break-even cost that year, I figured, was about 75 bushels. We had no crop insurance back then, and the only insurance programs we knew about were so bad, that if we had it, we would have been no better off. Hog prices were depressed that year, and we were losing about twenty dollars a head every time we went to market. In 1983, my cousin, John W. Watson died. We had been working closely together in the farming operation. We had a ripper bedder and he had planters, so we would rip and bed his land, and he would plant ours. We were at a fork in the road; we either had to quit farming or increase production. Up until this point, we had been farming about 65 acres of peanuts and 150 acres of corn along with having 100 purebred sows. We managed to get financing and increased our acreage. We were now farming around 600 acres, and we had added 25 head of cattle to go with our 100 sows. We tried different crops, such as soybeans, wheat, and grain sorghum along with our peanuts, trying to find the best moneymaker. What seemed like the thing to be in one year would turn out to be a disaster the next, but even through all of that, we seemed to be making progress. We were able to keep up our equipment and whittle down our debt to Production Credit Association. Even with the increase in production, it took nine years to pay off our 1980 debt.

Along with the everyday work, we also had worries of health issues to deal with. In 1985, my mother had to undergo her third open-heart surgery. She had her first in 1969 at Emory University Hospital, in Atlanta, Georgia. In those days, that was one of the few places in the country that heart surgery was performed. She could not even sit up by herself for six months after the surgery. That one was really hard on her, but she was young and tough. In 1975, she had her second. They replaced one of her heart valves with a valve from a pig. The procedure had improved a great deal, and by the time she had her third open heart surgery in 1985, she had become a pro at it.

In the late 70's and early 80's, I was in my twenties, with no college degree, and when you are working fourteen hours a day, seven days a week, it is difficult, to say the least, to go back to school. I needed ten credit hours to have an Associates Degree in agriculture, with which, if I had it and twenty-five cents, I could probably get a cup of coffee.

Even though I had some good times during these years and I met some true friends for life, these were also some of my darkest years. My college sweetheart had broken off our engagement, and my hurt permeated my entire being, affecting everything and everyone with whom I came in contact. My heart was darkened, and my mind was clouded. I was lonely, but I did not want to be hurt again, so I began to play the game. I hid my hurt, acted as if I did not care, and used others before they used me. When the hurt became too much to hide, I could drink a six-pack or two for temporary relief. With this method I found relief the next morning, too, because I would then be more concerned with my hurting head than my hurting heart. Even though the hurting in my heart might sometimes subside, the loneliness and emptiness did not.

We are not told how long it took the prodigal son to get back to his father. Some step right out of the hog pen onto a non-stop fast train right to the throne room of God. Some go by car, coach line, or horseback. I went on foot, questioning, wondering, pondering each step of the way. I questioned whether God could forgive me, wondered if he would, and pondered why he would. I stood in the pigpen of sin a while, just looking to the outside, before ever stepping out. Who knows, I may have never stepped out if God had not sent someone to walk out with me. By the way, God has already answered all those questions. He loves you so much he even had it put in writing. The document is available for you to read, so you can see for yourself. It is called the Holy Bible.

Deep inside I hated that I could be hurting others, so I stopped dating, and buried myself in work. I had about given up on getting married. I was a broke hog farmer, in his late twenties, who had to work fourteen hours a day. Who would want to be tied down to that? Sometimes, just for a change of pace, I would drive over to a bar in Dothan, Alabama. I would find a corner table, against the wall, where I would just sit. I would not drink much; that would only make work harder the next day. I would just sit for a couple of hours, and then go home. Doug, a guy I had come to know at some livestock shows, was sitting with me one night when a group of ladies came in. One of them had gone to high school with Doug, so she came over to say hello. Little did I know that she would be holding my hand as this prodigal son took his journey home. The word *wrong* would describe both of our lives at the time. I have always heard that two wrongs do not make a right, but what people forget is that "*...with God all things are possible.*" (Mat. 19:26) I could not imagine that this young lady would want to spend her life with a broke farm boy. I was through playing games, so I told her how much I was in debt, and I did not have much to offer her. This was the first time in my life that I had tried to talk a lady out of having a relationship with me. I thank God that I could not. Tammie and I were married on February 15, 1986. There was no doubt in our minds that God had brought us together. We decided it was time we got to know him better. We began to read our Bible more and talk to one another about God's word. We were on our journey back to the father's house.

The 1990's were not good years for agriculture. Droughts, floods, low farm commodity prices, rising labor costs, you name it, we had it. The Corps of Engineers rescinded our irrigation rights in 1990, and we had a towable center pivot irrigation system that we could water 240 acres with, sitting idol. We finally gave up the struggle and sold the system in 1995. Did I mention that was after it had been hit by a tornado, turned upside down, and had been removed from the field? We also raised purebred hogs, and after the packing plant closed in Georgia, the market dropped drastically. We sold males and females for others to use to produce hogs for slaughter, but when the slaughter market is down, no one buys breeding animals, so most of our breeding animals went to slaughter at very poor prices. Our farm has always been labor intensive, and with the rising cost of labor, good help was hard to find, so that translated into longer hours for us.

I now found myself in my thirties, still with no Associates Degree, which if I had it I could now use it to buy a cup of coffee if I had fifty cents to go along with it. My plan for a bright, successful career in agriculture seemed to be getting dimmer by the minute. The journey was long, but in the mid 90's I could see the lights from the father's house. I was getting closer, and I could now recognize there were times when God was working in my life and revealing things to me. That helped a lot when mother had her fourth open heart surgery in 1995. God gave me comfort and the knowledge that she would be all right, even though she stayed in the hospital for a month and had several complications. This time she had two valves replaced, one with a mechanical valve and another with a porcine valve. Her heart rate was too slow so they installed a pacemaker to keep her pumped up. She is a little older now, but she is still one tough lady. Dad has always said that she was tougher than he because he could have never gone through what she went through. Some think my mother is sickly and weak; how wrong they are. She is one of the strongest people I know, and she has been an inspiration to me. As a matter of fact, this book was her idea. The thought of mom having her 4th open heart surgery was weighing heavy on my dad. It was not only the stress that she would have to endure it, but how would he ever pay for it. When the doctor told mom and dad that they were recommending another heart surgery, dad told them to do whatever it took to make mom better. I guess the doctor could see the worry in dad's eyes and so he asked, "Are you worried about paying for this surgery?" Dad responded, "There is no way I can pay for this, but do whatever it takes and I will send you whatever I can as often as I can". The doctor told us that mom had been under the care of Emory University Hospital for years and that he felt they owed her this surgery, so there would be no charge. The doctor's response gave dad some peace of mind. We were in bad need of a pickup truck as the one we had was not very road worthy for any long distance. When dad was told that mom's surgery would be at no cost, dad nervously decided to get a truck. He had finally settled down with the decision he had made; that is until the 180 thousand dollar bill came in from the hospital. I thought dad was going to have to have heart surgery! I assured him it had to be a mistake and encouraged him to call the doctor. He did and the doctor apologized and said that it should never have happened. The doctor sent us a letter to send back with the bill explaining there was no charge. Thank you Lord!

Yes, it was a long journey, and my wife and I were growing closer to the Lord every day. Then on February 11, 1996, my wife and I felt the heavenly Father's arms around us, and we knew, without a shadow of a doubt, that we were forgiven. There may be people on this earth who will never forgive us, but God has, and that makes all the difference. We no longer wonder about our salvation, whether or not we will make it to heaven. We know that Christ has a place for us. *In my father's house are many mansions, if it were not so I would have told you. I go to prepare a place for you. And if I go and prepare a place for you, I will come again and receive you to myself; that where I am, there you may be also.* (John 14:2-3)

The prodigal son in the scripture had turned away from a life of sin and had turned toward the way of righteousness. There had been true repentance in his heart. The son had done more than state his belief; his words were now affecting his lifestyle. Yes, he still reeked with the odor of sin. Many times, even after we have changed our lifestyle, we are still left with the consequences of our past sin. But praise God! How wonderful he is, for he loves us anyway.

The Bible says that the father had compassion on his son. I think many times in our society that we read that word lightly. In our language, it means to have sympathetic consciousness of other's distress, together with a desire to alleviate it. The Greek word seems to have a deeper meaning. It means not only to have pity or sympathy, but it means to yearn for, and it comes from another word meaning to have inward affection and tender mercy.

That does sound very much like our Father in heaven, does it not? He has sympathy and pity for our fallen condition. He knows we cannot alleviate it ourselves; he loves us so much and longs to have us with him that he extends his tender mercy toward us, if we will just take that step toward him, as the prodigal son did.

Sometimes people think that they are too far away from God; that they will never be able to have a close relationship with Christ because they are so deep in sin. They think that God could not love them; they have done too much wrong. They think they have committed the unpardonable sin.

Here we have a picture of a son who had turned from the father and lived a life of sin. He had gone against everything his father had taught him and basically made a mockery of his former life. Yet, when the father saw him, he ran to him, fell on his neck, and kissed him. He did not wait until the son was on the front porch with his hat in his hand. He did not say to him, "I told you so," or scold him for squandering away his fortune. He went out to meet him. He did not go to chastise him but to show him how much he loved him.

If you have ever started to go to someone to apologize for hurting their feelings or doing them wrong in some way, you know that the last mile, the last block, or the last hundred yards can be the hardest part of the trip. We start out encouraged and strengthened by the fact that we are doing the right thing. On the way, Satan always seems to show up with a list of what ifs. What if they hate you anyway? What if you make things worse than they already are? What if? What if? What if? I think that is why God, like the father in the parable, comes to meet us while we are still far-off. He comes to strengthen us for the last leg of the journey. We do not have to walk the last mile alone; he will lead us home.

Chapter 8

Luke 15:21 And the son said to him, "Father, I have sinned against heaven and in your sight, and am no longer worthy to be called your son."

Repentance is more than feeling convicted and saying I am sorry. We are to act upon these convictions. If the son had said, "I'm sorry," but stayed in the hog pen, he would be no better off. He would still be unable to receive the blessings that the father had for him. He had to take a step out in faith, a step out of the hog pen and into the presence of the father.

By stepping out of the pigpen, by taking action, the son made a public statement of his faith. The Bible says that we are to confess our sin publicly. *Confess your trespasses to one another, and pray for one another, that you may be healed.* (James 5:16) That does not necessarily mean to go into every detail of our sin. If we are not careful, we may be giving Satan the glory for our pitfalls. We also must be sure not to confess the sins of others publicly. That is their job not ours. People tend to not want to show their faults without showing the faults of others.

By stepping out of the pigpen, and following Christ, we are confessing God's lordship over us. The son said, "*I am no longer worthy to be called your son; make me like one of your hired servants.*"

(Luke 15:19) There are people who wish to slide in the back door of the church, quietly take a seat, and be insured of a place in heaven. They are not willing to publicly confess Jesus as their Lord and Savior. Some have not even come to accept the fact that they need a Savior. They do not realize that their sin has separated them from God. They think they are living a good life; they are depending on their own righteousness. That is not a good idea, for the Bible says," *But we are all as an unclean thing, and all our righteousnesses are as filthy rags; and we all do fade as a leaf; and our iniquities, like the wind, have taken us away.*" (Isaiah 64:6)

No matter how good we think our life is, when we stand before a pure and holy God, our righteousness is like filthy rags. We all need a Savior, and that Savior must be the very sinless, Son of God, Jesus Christ. Jesus said, "*No man cometh unto the father, but by me.*" (John 14:6) We must accept Jesus Christ as our Lord and Savior, and we must do it publicly. Now there is some good churchy language for you! Some may not understand those words. When we say we are accepting Jesus, we are actually saying we are accepting God's provision for our salvation. What actually happens is this. We trust Jesus, submit to His authority, follow Him, and He accepts us! We then become part of His Body on earth and because of our submission to Him we receive the Holy Spirit into our heart and life to lead and be our guide. This is our first act of repentance as we turn away from the sin that we are aware of and turn to Jesus, our savior and God's provision for our salvation! There will be more repenting along the way as the Lord reveals things to us that He desires to change. Martin Luther put it something like this, "The Christian life is a life of repentance". Some say that I am adding works to salvation. No, if you are truly saved; you are following the savior, because He is your master, and He said, "*Repent for the Kingdom of Heaven is at hand*". (Mat. 4:17) How can He be your Lord, Master, Savior, if you if you refuse to obey and follow Him?

Answer: He is not! It is very true that our confession of Christ must be done publicly. There are no such things as Camouflage Christians. *Whosoever therefore shall confess me before men, him will I confess also before my father which is in heaven. But whosoever shall deny me before men, him will I also deny before my father which is in heaven.* (Mat. 10:32-33) Some preachers and teachers who are more interested in filling the pews in their respective congregations than they are about getting people into the kingdom of God, would tell you that those scriptures do not mean you will not go to Heaven, only that you will not be acknowledged to receive blessings here on earth! That is heresy that has been brought into the church! It is the stuff that the Pharisees are dragging their robes through (mentioned in earlier chapters) as they walk through the pigpen of life! If Jesus is your only way to Heaven, (and He is – John 14:6) He calls you to repent and follow Him, (and He does – Mat. 4:17) if Jesus says we should put Him above all our earthly possessions, (and He does – Lk. 18:22) even above our own family, (and He does – Mat. 10:37) then He really means, "*If you deny me before men, I will deny you before my Father in Heaven*". Since Jesus is your only access to Heaven – you will not enter! Like all Satan's lies that have crept into the church, there is always some element of truth. Though *God causes the sun to rise on the evil and the good and sends the rain on the just and the unjust,* (Mat. 5:45 some blessings only come by acknowledging God and His ways and being obedient to Him. (Is. 1:19) Salvation is not that hard; just trust Jesus, and follow Him; but many preachers and teachers today make it too easy in order to fill their earthly buildings. Just repeat this prayer after me and you will be saved. Many repeat the prayer and continue to live their lives as before with no change what so ever. There are many who live with a false sense of security. They enter into the sanctuary every week but will not make it to a heavenly home.

In the days in which we live, it could be said that confessing Christ is the hardest, easiest thing a person could ever do. In our country we are not persecuted for our faith. Though we may be ridiculed by some of the porcine species, generally our lives are not threatened. When a confession for Christ is made, it is usually made in a church surrounded by people who care about you and, many times, are praying for you. Many of those people who surround you have been where you are, and they know how it feels to have that burden of sin lifted from them. They cannot describe it to you. It is something you have to experience for yourself, and they want you to have that experience.

As the hymn of invitation starts to play, the war between principalities and powers of heaven and the underworld rage in a conflict that is beyond our comprehension. The battle for your soul becomes fierce as the Holy Spirit fires conviction, Satan shields with pride. The Holy Spirit offers forgiveness, and Satan confuses with questions. The Holy Spirit suggests a plea bargain of repentance, and Satan blows a smokescreen of doubt.

The battle for your soul you may not see, but the results you can feel in your body. Every muscle in your body begins to tense. Adrenalin starts pumping and mixed signals are being fired to your brain, one telling you to move, and the other shouting freeze. Your heart rate is escalating, and you feel as if your air source is depleting. There is what feels like a knot, the size of a softball in your throat, and one the size of a football in your stomach. The tendons in your hands contract as you grip the back of the pew in front of you, harder and harder until your knuckles have now turned white. There are only two ways to bring the battle to a close. One is the last stanza of the song and the benediction. If you can hold on until then, you know the onslaught will subside, but then you have that empty wasted feeling inside to deal with. That feeling will remain until the next major battle for your soul begins.

There is another way to end the onslaught. It is the way of repentance. Give in to the Holy Spirit, step out in faith, put your whole trust in Christ, walk down that aisle and surrender your heart to Jesus. Do this, and you will feel the sweet release from your guilt, and it will bring an end to the wasteland in your heart. If you will allow him, the empty, barren place inside you will be filled with the very spirit of God. You see, it should be very easy to put your trust in the very one who created you; to walk twenty feet, stand in front of a group of people who love you, and say, "I trust Jesus and I want to live for him." The outside restrictions make it easy; it is the inner battle that makes it hard. So hard, yet so easy—the hardest, easiest thing you will ever do!

The son in the parable did not even get to finish his confession before the father interrupted him. You might wonder why the father did not listen to the son. You see, the father knew the son's heart. Our Father is all-seeing and all-knowing. It was a long journey from the pigpen to the father's home. I am sure he had rehearsed his speech in his mind many times. The Father in heaven hears every rehearsal. The father was expecting him; he was watching for him. How else would he have recognized him when the son "...was yet a great way off?" The father knew that the son had a repentant heart, and he had come to meet him, to walk him home. When you have a repentant heart, you will never walk alone.

The son told the father that he had sinned against heaven and in his sight. We sometimes think that our way of life is our business; that it does not affect anyone else. Our sin not only affects us, but everyone and everything around us, just as the sin of Adam in the Garden of Eden affected the entire creation. God told Adam that because of his sin the ground would be cursed. *Cursed is the ground for thy sake; in sorrow shalt thou eat of it all the days of thy life.* (Gen. 3:17)

It not only happened that way in the beginning, but the principle is still the same. *If my people, which are called by my name, shall humble themselves, and pray, and seek my face, and turn from their wicked ways; then will I hear from heaven, and will forgive their sin, and will heal their land.* (2 Chronicles 7:14) There is a lot of talk these days about the crazy weather we have. Extreme seasons, they always seem too hot or too cold, too wet or too dry. Today everyone is talking about Climate Change and how to fix it. Climate Change is the very least of the problems in our country. There will always be those who will live totally and blatantly against the Word of God, but when a country starts passing laws that are contrary to God's Word, the country is asking for judgment! Our country has become corrupt! Our land needs healing!

Humbling ourselves is an obligation where we have become very weak. Yes, I did say obligation. We are obligated to do this in order for our land to be healed and have our sins forgiven. {See previous scripture} I had been attending my church for 35 years before I saw anyone go to the altar, get on his or her knees, and pray. We have become more afraid of what the person on the end of the pew will think of us than what God thinks of us. We are afraid someone will think we have done something wrong. If we have studied our Bible, we know we have. *For it is written, there is none righteous, no, not one.* (Rom. 3:10) David said it in Ps. 14 and Ps. 53. Solomon said it in Ecl. 7:20, and it is still true today. During 35 years, some people should have felt the need to humble themselves and get on their knees. If we do not feel the need to humble ourselves for our own sake, why don't we humble ourselves for the needs of others? What about your friends and family who need Jesus to guide them in their lives? If you cannot think of anyone else to pray for, pray for me. I need the prayers and you need the practice. Who knows? When you find yourself in that humble position, God may reveal something to you about your life that you need to pray about. What better place is there to do that than God's house! The reason I did not humble myself, I now realize, was because I was still in the hog pen. What is your excuse, and when will your excuses end?

Another area where we have fallen short is in seeking God's face. Work and recreation have become top priorities and seeking God is somewhere at the bottom of the list, if it is on our list at all. There is an old hymn written by Lida Shivers Leech named "Trust, Try, and Prove Me." It is based on a scripture in Malachi. *Bring ye all the tithes into the storehouse, that there may be meat in mine house, and prove me now herewith, saith the lord of hosts, if I will not open you the windows of heaven, and pour you out a blessing, that there shall not be room enough to receive it.* (Malachi 3:10) This is the way the first verse goes:

> Bring ye all the tithes into the store-house,
> All your money, talents, <u>time</u>, and love—

Some of us may tithe our money, and some of us may be using our talents for God. Many of us are not; I could name some names here, but I will not be tacky. If God has given you a talent, you should be using it for his glory. If not, he may decide to take it away from you. Jesus told a parable in Matthew, chapter 25, about a master who was going on a long journey, so he gave his servants differing amounts of talents. To one servant he gave five talents; to another he gave two; to another he gave one. Jesus uses money in the parable to make a point, but the Greek word for *talent* is *talanton*, pronounced *tal'-an-ton*, meaning neuter of a presumed derivative of the original form, which could mean any number of things that the master desired to give. Those in the parable who used their talents wisely were blessed, but the one who hid his talent, from him his talent was taken. If God has given you a talent, and he has, find out what it is and use it for his glory.

We might be tithing our money, talents and love, but what about our time? Are you spending a tenth of your time with God in prayer and Bible study? If you are tithing your time and you are in your mid-twenties, you should have your doctorate degree by now. The truth is, we do not spend enough time with our master, seeking to know him, seeking to understand his ways, seeking his face.

I have found that the more time I spend with God, the more I come to know him. The more we know about God, his ways, and his plan for our life the more he can use us. It is funny though. The more you know about God's ways, the more you realize you do not know. God's wisdom and righteousness are infinite. If you love the Lord, you will desire to know him. Jesus said, "*Blessed are those who hunger and thirst for righteousness, for they shall be filled.*" (Mat. 5:6)

The last credential we must meet in order for God to forgive our sins and heal our land is repentance. I have seen people become humble; I have seen people pray; and I have seen people studying the scriptures, supposedly seeking God. But if we fail to turn from our wicked ways, it is all for naught. We must change our thinking; we must change our direction; and we must repent.

In order to draw closer to God, we must change our direction. We must stop being worldly-minded and become spiritually-minded. If we would tithe our money, talents, love, and most of all our time, we would become more spiritually-minded. We cannot please God by thinking only of today and ourselves. *For they that are after the flesh do mind the things of the flesh, but they that are after the spirit the things of the spirit.* (Rom. 8:5) The Bible says, "*Those who are in the flesh cannot please God.*" (Rom. 8:8) How do I know if I am in the flesh, or after the flesh, you might ask? Well let's let the scripture give us the answer to that. *Now the works of the flesh are evident, which are: adultery, fornication, uncleanness, lewdness, idolatry, sorcery, hatred, contentions, jealousies, outburst of wrath, selfish ambitions, dissensions, heresies, envy, murders, drunkenness, revelries, and the like; of which I tell you beforehand, just as I also told you in time past, that those who practice such things will not inherit the kingdom of God.* (Gal. 5:19-21) Let us look at those a little closer in case there is some misunderstanding. Adultery: sexual relations outside the confines of marriage ordained by God. Fornication: any immoral sexual activity with anything or anybody outside of God's ordained marital relationship. Uncleanness: and physical or moral impurities. Lewdness: foul language or gestures. Idolatry: Any thing, any place, or any person you place ahead of God. Sorcery: sometimes translated witchcraft and conjures up ideas of demon or underworld worship but is actually more than that. The Greek word is pharmakeia. It is where we get our word pharmacy, meaning those who practice drug use. Hatred: It says in 1 John 3:15 that whoever hates his brother is a murderer. Contentions: means controversy and disputes. Jesus said reconcile even before you make an offering to the Lord in Mathew 5: 23-24. Jealousies: resentful or bitter. Outburst of wrath: It says in James 3:6 that the tongue is a fire, a world of iniquity. Selfish ambitions: Selfishness is the heart of all sin. It is all about me. It is I who deserves it all. Remember I is the center of all SIN! Dissensions: is a difference of opinion that causes strife within a group. When it comes to God's will, His Word, and His way, our opinion is not important. It is what God says that matters. Heresies: an opinion that goes against God's Word. Refer back to the last few sentences. Envy: is resentment aroused by the desire for possessions or qualities of another. It is coveting on steroids, and the Bible says thou shalt not covet. Murders- this is where most people will say, I've done a lot wrong but I haven't killed anybody; but the Bible says *Everyone who hates his brother is a murderer.* (1 John 3:15) Revelries: To take great pleasure and delight in the Biblical sense meaning while railing, chiding, or taunting another. The scripture goes on to say and things like this that I have told you about beforehand, or before now. I have heard people say, "Well the Bible only mentioned that one or two times". How many times does God have to say something before it counts? I'll give you a hint. My earthly father would say, "I'm not going to tell you again". The interpretation of that was when I say it once, I mean it, and if you don't believe me – try me, correction will come and it would come quickly and decisively! God must be serious about this because he stated similar things several times. *Do you not know that the unrighteous will not inherit the kingdom of God? Do not be deceived. Neither fornicators, nor idolaters, nor adulterers nor homosexuals, nor sodomites, nor thieves, nor covetous, nor drunkards, nor revilers, nor extortioners will inherit the kingdom of God.* (1 Cor. 6:9-10) There is another list in Revelation 21:8. I'm sure as you read these lists that there are some things that will make everyone of us uncomfortable to say the least, unless you are a Proverbs 12:1 kind of person. I'll let you look that one up. The King James may not make it quite clear to you, so I will suggest you read the New King James. It puts in the language you will definitely understand. I'm glad 1 Corinthians chapter six did not end with verse 10. If there is breath in you, it is not the end. There is hope. *And such were some of you, but you were washed, but you were sanctified, but you were justified in the name of the Lord Jesus and by the Spirit of our God.* (1 Cor.6: 11)

The son in the parable had come home, and the father was about to open the windows of heaven and pour out blessings that he would not have room enough to receive. Are you ready to come home and receive the blessings God has in store for you?

Chapter 9

Luke 15: 22 But the father said to his servants, "Bring out the best robe and put it on him, and put a ring on his hand and sandals on his feet."

When a child of God repents and turns back to God, you can be sure that God will be there. God does not make you live in a strain, wondering whether or not you will be received. God, through the power of the Holy Spirit, will come and meet you and walk with you all the way to the pearly gates of home. God will do more than be with you, he will bless you, and he will adorn you with gifts, just as he did with the son in this parable. This is also true for someone who has turned to God for the first time. The presence of the Holy Spirit abiding with you and the blessings of God are available to you, if you will just accept them. Let us take a closer look at some of the gifts God will bestow upon us.

The father said to his servants to bring out the best robe and put it on his son. The robe represents the covering that God has provided for our sin. Isaiah speaks of it as a robe of righteousness or a garment of salvation. *I will greatly rejoice in the lord, my soul shall be joyful in my God; for he has clothed me with the garments of salvation, he has covered me with the robe of righteousness.* (Isaiah 61:10) Our salvation, our purification, it is all a gift from God. God provided the way for our salvation and purification from before the beginning of the world, as we know it. In Revelation, the thirteenth chapter, it speaks of the lamb slain from the foundation of the world.

God's plan of salvation for mankind was not an afterthought; it was his plan from the start. God knew that man would give in to temptation. Here is where someone always asks, "If God knew we were going to sin if He gave us a choice, why did He make us that way"? The reason is because love can only be expressed when there is a choice not to love. If there is no choice, it is not love! Yes, God could have made us different. He could have made us with the ability to never sin; but he wanted us to have a choice, so he gave us free will, and his desire is for us to choose him. He will not force you to choose him, follow him, or love him. It is your decision, but he has paid the way for you to come to him. God bought you a ticket to heaven with the sacrifice of his only begotten son. What better way for God to express His love toward us than to give His best to redeem us at our worst. *But God demonstrates His own love toward us, in that while we were still sinners, Christ died for us.* (Rom. 5:8) God did not give his best to leave you at your worst. He wants better for you! God accepts you as you are but He loves you too much to let you stay that way. If you belong to Him, He will change you! He will change you as you follow Christ! Follow Him! He will lead you to Heaven; He has your ticket waiting for you at the gate!

God is holy, and he demands that his people be holy. The only way we can become holy and acceptable before God is through Jesus Christ. We are shown all through the New Testament that the shed blood of Jesus, the sinless Son of God, "*washes us from our sin,*" (Rev. 1:5) and "*cleanses of from our sin.*" (1 John 1:7) The blood of Jesus not only washes and cleanses us of our sin, it also redeems us. His blood paid for our sin. (Eph. 1:7; 1 Pet. 1:18-19; Col. 1:14)

By his blood we are also justified before God. (Rom. 5:8) We are made right before God. It is just as if we never sinned. His blood sanctifies us. (Heb. 13:12) We are made holy before God. We are "*...reconciled by the blood of Jesus,*" (Col. 1:20) and God can now accept us. The Bible tells us that we are "*...brought near*" to God by the blood of Jesus. (Eph. 2:13)

In the Old Testament, we see the prophets foreseeing the coming of Christ for the redemption of man. Jesus Christ took the sin of man upon himself. The spotless lamb, the perfect Son of God, the one who knew no sin, bore our sin on the cross of Calvary. *Surely he has borne our griefs and carried our sorrows.* (Isaiah 53:4) He paid the price for our sin. *He was wounded for our transgressions, he was bruised for our iniquities; the chastisement for our peace was upon him, and by his stripes we are healed.* (Isaiah 53:5) When Jesus hung on the cross, our sin was imputed to him, and the Bible says in Romans, chapter four, that through faith in him, his righteousness was imputed to us. Jesus took our sin upon him so that we might put on his robe of righteousness, his garment of salvation.

Not only is this robe of Jesus a righteous robe, it is a royal, priestly robe. During the Old Testament times, ordinary people could not go before God to make request or ask forgiveness for their sin. The high priest had to be an intercessor for them. Once a year, the priest would enter the innermost chamber, called the Holy of Holies, and make a sacrifice for the sins of the people. A veil or curtain separated the Holy of Holies from the rest of the temple. When Christ died on the cross, the veil was ripped from top to bottom. *Then behold the veil of the temple was torn in two from top to bottom; and the earth quaked. And the rocks were split.* (Mat. 27:51) Now everyone has access to God through his son Jesus, who now sits at the right hand of the Father to make intercession for us. We no longer have to go through an earthly priest, for Christ

"*...has made us kings and priests to his God and father.*" (Rev. 1:6) In order to receive this priesthood, you must have faith in Jesus, and your first prayer must be a prayer of repentance, for without repentance there is no forgiveness, and without forgiveness there is no refreshing for the soul. *Repent therefore and be converted, that your sins may be blotted out, so that times of refreshing may come from the presence of the lord.* (Acts 3:19) Some may offer prayers to God without repentance, but their words will go unheard. *And when ye spread forth your hands, I will hide mine eyes from you: yea, when ye make many prayers, I will not hear; your hands are full of blood.* (Isaiah 1:15) Some may shout of their innocence, but we are all guilty because it was for our sin that Jesus was slain, not his. He took our stripes, our bruises, our insults, our ridicule, our cross, and he let us go free. Will you turn to God and accept the robe of righteousness, the garment of salvation that he offers to you? You have a free paid ticket to heaven. Will you use it, or will you pay your own way to hell with your sin? *If we say that we have no sin, we deceive ourselves, and the truth is not in us.* (1 John 1:8)

After the father had told his servants to put the best robe upon him, they were told to put a ring on his finger. In Bible times, the ring usually carried a signet or a family seal. The ring was a sign that he belonged to the family. After the son returned to the father, after he had been cleansed, when he was adorned with the robe of righteousness, he was then sealed by the presence of the Holy Spirit. *In him you also trusted, after you heard the word of truth, the gospel of your salvation; in whom also, having believed, you were sealed with the Holy Spirit of promise.* (Eph. 1:13-14) Jesus promised when he left this world that he would send the Holy Spirit to comfort and guide us. Jesus said that the Holy Spirit would not only be with us but would reside in us to fill that emptiness inside us that we all are longing to fill. *And I will pray the father and he will give you another helper that he may abide with you forever, the spirit of truth, whom the world cannot receive, because it neither sees him nor knows him; but you know him for he dwells with you and will be in you.* (John 14:16-17) These are some of the gifts you receive when you fully surrender your life to the King of Kings and Lord of Lords. This occurs in the Justification process. You are now justified before God. God had imparted the righteousness of Jesus upon you. In simple language you may now stand before God justified, **(Just if I'd) never sinned.** This is only the beginning. The Holy Spirit who now dwells within you will begin to change you, to be conformed into the image of Jesus Christ. (Rom. 8:29) This is the sanctification process as He sets you apart as *His workmanship, created in Christ Jesus for good works, which God prepared beforehand that we should walk in them.* (Eph. 2:10)

It is the Holy Spirit that indwells believers, that gives a person the ability to live as God would have them live. It is the Holy Spirit that God works through to change a person, and it is only by the power of the Holy Spirit that a person can truly be changed. The Holy Spirit first convicts us of our sin from the outside. As we submit to the conviction, he indwells and seals us with forgiveness and righteousness, but he does not stop there. The more we submit ourselves to God, the more power we receive from the Holy Spirit. God's power is shown more through our weakness. *My grace is sufficient for you, for my strength is made perfect in weakness.* (2 Cor. 12:9)

Too many times we resist the spirit and try to work for the Lord in our own strength, and no one is impressed. God does not want you to work for him; he wants to work through you. He wants you to do things that are beyond your ability, and you can, through the power of the Holy Spirit. All through the Bible we see how God used ordinary people to do miraculous things. A young shepherd boy killed a giant that caused an entire army to shake in its tracks. Another shepherd led millions of Israelites across a wilderness to a land of promise, and a small group of fishermen turned the world upside down by spreading the gospel of Jesus Christ. Guess what? God still does it the same way today. Our problems and giants in life may be different, but the solution is still the same. Submit your weakness to God and let his power be made known through it. Your giant may be overcoming an addiction or a fear to do the job God has for you. The power of the Holy Spirit can carry you over, or carry you through, any problem you may face. Submission to the will, presence, and power of the Holy Spirit will change your life.

There was a time in my life when I was terrified to stand in front of a crowd and talk about my Lord and Savior. I started out singing in church. That in itself was a miracle, and I would try to introduce the song I was going to sing. I would try and tell why the song meant so much to me or quote some scripture that seemed appropriate. My palms would sweat, my knees would shake, my lips would tremble, and my voice would crack. I would plan for hours on just one or two lines, and when the time came for me to stand up, my legs would feel like rubber.

One morning I was listed on the program to sing a special in my home church, and as the pastor was making announcements and taking prayer requests, I was arguing with God. I knew that God wanted me to say something about the song that I was going to sing, to encourage the congregation to listen to the words, and I was scared to death. As I sat in the choir loft, I was talking to God. I was saying, "God, you know I can't talk because I'll get nervous. I'll start shaking; my voice will crack; I'll cry; I'll make a mess; I just can't do it, and I'm not going to do it." My problem was that I had trusted Christ for my salvation, but at that moment, I was not allowing him to be lord of my life. I was not submitting to the power available through the Holy Spirit. I was doing the work of the Lord in my own power, and that did not amount to much.

When time came for me to sing, I did not speak; I just picked up the microphone, turned on the tape and started to sing. I knew what would be best for me to do, and I was going to do it my way, and God let me. Big mistake! Half way through the song, God took the words away from me. I had no idea what the words were. Not only did I not know the words, I had no idea even what the rest of the song was about. I went totally blank. God had brought me to a point of decision. I could run out the back door of the church, or I could trust God to give me, not only the words to say, but also the words of the song. I chose that very moment to trust God totally. I talked for three or four minutes that morning as God gave me the words to say. I could not tell you now what I said; I just spoke as God provided the word. At that moment, I knew what Jesus meant, when he told the disciples, "*Do not worry about how or what you should speak. For it will be given to you in that hour what you should speak; for it is not you who speak, but the spirit of your father who speaks in you.*" (Mat. 10:19-20) I started the tape over and I still had no idea what the rest of the song was, but I had learned that I could trust God to give it to me if I needed it. As I was singing, I was praying, "Lord, I am trusting you to give me the rest of the words to the song." I was half way through the song and still no words for the last half. There was a downbeat in the song where the second half started. When the downbeat came, so did the words. If we will follow God, he will provide the way. The name of the song was "If You Died Tonight." There were many people who came to me after the service and said, "I was enjoying the song, but I was not really listening to the words until you stopped and spoke." God knew how it should be done all along, but he chose to do it through me. I still try to do things God's way. I never plan anything to say about a song; I just try to follow the spirit and let him do the talking. It surely works a lot smoother that way.

The Holy Spirit can change you, shape you, mold you, and make you into more than you can ever hope to be on your own. The Holy Spirit can remove fear and give you a boldness to witness for Christ. He can take an average "C" high school student, who never cared for school, allow him to earn a master's degree in Christian ministry, with a 3.9 GPA, and go on to finish his Doctorate in Christian Ministry. The Holy Spirit can touch an old country boy's voice and change the sound before it reaches the ears of those who hear it so that it can touch their hearts. The Holy Spirit can whisper the words to a gospel song in the ear of a farm boy as he writes them down on a paper sack that will later be recorded and sung to give glory to God. The Holy Spirit can lead someone who knows absolutely nothing about music to record six gospel tapes and several CD's. The Holy Spirit can help a redneck, who cannot read his own handwriting when it is cold, write a book, in hope that someone else may have a closer walk with God. These are just a few of the things that I happen to know that God can do, because he did it through me.

We notice in the scripture that the father said to put sandals on his son's feet. This reminds me of the scriptures in the sixth chapter of Ephesians, where it describes the whole armor of God. It tells us to "*...shod your feet with the preparation of the gospel of peace.*" (Eph. 6:15) As the father placed sandals of the feet of this wayward son who had returned home, he was truly shod. He had experienced the gospel of peace first hand. He knew how it felt to have peace with God. He knew first hand of the gospel, the good news, that one can be reconciled to God, and when one has peace with God he begins to become more peaceful with his fellow man. The fruit of the spirit will begin to show in his life. *The fruit of the spirit is love, joy, peace, longsuffering, kindness, goodness, faithfulness, gentleness, self-control.* (Gal. 5:22-23) Would you like to receive all these blessings that God is waiting to give you? The choice is yours. It all starts with repentance.

Chapter 10

Luke 15:23-24 And bring the fatted calf here and kill it, and let us eat and be merry; for this my son was dead and is alive again; he was lost and is found. And they began to be merry.

This is a perfect example of the joy in heaven as a lost soul comes to know the Lord, whether it is a first time experience or a return home. *Likewise, I say to you, there is joy in the presence of the angels of God over one sinner who repents.* (Luke 15:10) The father brought out the best for his son, just as God offers the best for his children. God knows what will bring us the most pleasure, better than we know ourselves. All of heaven rejoices when a sinner turns to the Lord; and our heavenly Father, if you will allow him, will prepare for you a feast beyond your wildest imagination.

Now that the son had returned home, he also had the blessing of a family to nurture, love, and support him, just as a Christian family should nurture, love, and support a brother or sister in Christ. Through our faith in Jesus Christ, we become united together as a family. We become brothers and sisters in Christ; we become children of God when we allow the Holy Spirit to enter our lives and hearts. It is by the presence of the Holy Spirit that we know we are truly God's children. *You received the spirit of adoption by whom we cry out, "Abba, Father." The Spirit himself bears witness with our spirit that we are children of God.* (Rom. 8:15-16) What does it mean to cry Abba Father? Abba is an Aramaic word for father and is used 3 times in scripture. Most Bible teachers have said in the past that the word Abba was an endearing term, holding more intimacy than father and therefore would be better translated daddy. While this is very true, I believe it also holds a deeper meaning. The word comes hear in verse 15 just after verse 14 has told us that true son's of God are those who are led by the Spirit of God. Those who are led by the Spirit are obedient to the Spirit. Another place the word Abba is used is in Mark 14:36 when Jesus is in the Garden of Gethsemane as He prayed, "*Abba Father, all things are possible for you. Take this cup away from Me; nevertheless, not what I will, but what you will.*" It is not only a term of endearment but a term of obedience! Not my will but thy will be done! Respect and obedience to fathers is something that is rare and even frowned upon in society today, but it was something that was expected and rewarded when I was young. The other place this term is used is Galatians 4:6, *and because you are sons, God has sent forth the Spirit of His Son into your hearts, crying out, "Abba Father!"* Again it is the Spirit of Christ, the Spirit of God that you are led by, makes you a son, which allows you to have this close relationship to the father that you desire to be obedient to. In the context of the scriptures it is used in we must understand that it is not only daddy, but a daddy you love and are obedient to!

When we become children of God, we become brothers and sisters with Christ and with our fellow Christians. *And if children, then heirs, heirs of God, and joint heirs with Christ.* (Rom. 8:17)

Not only have we become a family body, but we also have become a part of the body of Christ. *So we, being many, are one body in Christ, and every one members of one another.* (Rom. 12:5) As a part of the body of Christ we all have been given gifts, special duties to do, in order that the body might function properly.

Whatever gift God has given us we should use it joyfully to the glory of God. We must not be jealous of other Christian's gifts or think that we are not important or not useful because we do not have the gifts that others have. All parts of the body must do their jobs in order for the body to function. If one body part does not function, it affects the entire body. *And whether one member suffer, all the members suffer with it; or one member honored, all members rejoice with it.* (1 Cor. 12:26) God does not call everyone to preach or teach; some may be called to serve, others to encourage, and others to be prayer warriors. Whatever God has called you to do, it is important to the body of Christ. One person is not more important to the body than the other. We need each other. *If the whole body were an eye, where would be the hearing? If the whole were hearing, where would be the smelling?* (1 Cor. 12:17) *And if they were all one member, where would the body be?* (1 Cor. 12:19) When the body is functioning properly and being led by the head, which is Christ, God's people will begin to see miraculous things happen. A properly functioning body of Christ should do the same things Christ did while he was on earth. *Verily, verily, I say unto you, he that believeth on me, the works that I do shall he do also; and greater works than these shall he do, because I go unto my father.* (John 14:12) If our church body is not seeing signs and wonders being done among us, it is because some of the body parts are not doing what they are called to do. How about you? Are you using the gifts God has provided for you or have you even discovered what your gifts are? Let me encourage you to find your gift or gifts and use them. You just may be the one holding up the production of God's work by the body.

Many people will try to use the excuse that a certain thing is not my gift when they don't feel comfortable doing that ministry. A number of years ago, there were people who even taught in churches that if you are not comfortable with a certain ministry that was a sign that it was not your gift, and you should stay away from it. That was one of the dumbest things I have ever heard. Everything God has ever called me to do was uncomfortable! Nothing that God calls you to do is going to be comfortable. He is calling you to do spiritual things, and you are a physical being. Unless you are born again you won't even have a desire to attempt spiritual things. One of our biggest problems is we want everything comfortable. We want to be liked by everyone. We want to be in control. We want ministry to be easy, and we have made our relationship with God way too comfortable. If you are telling the truth, you will not be liked by everyone. You are not in control, God is! Ministry is not easy but it is a blessing to get to see God in action, and you should never think that you are so buddy-buddy with the Lord that you can get your way when He says no. Refer back to the previous statement – you are not in control, God is! So what happens when a body is missing a part? In the physical body, when one part is missing the other parts enhance their action. If someone loses their eyesight, the hearing, smelling, and touch senses becomes enhanced in order to protect the body so the body can continue to function. So, when the door of ministry is opened to you, don't make excuses. You may be the one protecting the body or enabling it to continue in ministry. I personally am not sure what my gift is, but I do know this, if God opens a door of ministry for me, I can trust Him to prepare me for whatever He calls me to do. If God brought you to it – He will bring you through it! God does not call those who are able – He enables those He calls! Just listen to Him, trust Him, be obedient to Him, and follow Him!

Too many times when we attempt to come to God, we still try to run the show. We want to tell God just what we need, as if we knew. A young lady in high school or college thinks she just has to marry that jock on the football team. She thinks she just cannot live without him. She cannot see down the road ten years when he will have a sixty-pound beer belly and arthritic joints. A young man thinks the love of his life should look just like the cocktail waitress at the bar around the corner. He does not notice that she is an alcoholic with a three pack-a-day habit that would run through a fortune and leave him in the cold. We think God just does not understand. All the while, God is offering rib eye steak, and we are asking for franks and beans. God offers us a delicious, satisfying meal, and we are asking for something that will just give us gas pains. When we come to God, we need to let him make the decisions for us. The father has killed the fatted calf, and he is offering the best for us. We just need to thankfully accept it.

I once heard a man compare his wife to a meal. Read on, ladies, before you get upset. Someone asked him if he ever thought about cheating on his wife? He replied, "Why should I go out for hamburgers when I can have steak at home?" Coming from most men I know, that is about as powerful a compliment as I have ever heard, and that is certainly the way I feel about my wife.

I was in my late twenties when I finally found my mate for life. I had decided that I would probably never marry. Being a broke farmer, I was not a very good candidate, and all my picks, so far, had not worked out. In my search for a mate, I was spending a lot of time on a smorgasbord of tacos, burritos, and hot tamales. Very spicy, with lots of flavor to tantalize your taste buds, they would leave you with a tremendous amount of heartburn. I have heard all my life, "When the right one comes along, you will know it." What many people fail to realize is that the people who gave you this information were Godly people, and in order for you to know when the right one comes along, you must first have a relationship with the Lord. If you are listening to the Lord, he will let you know when it is right. When I met my wife, I was not listening, but I was questioning. When I could not talk God out of it, I tried to talk

Tammie out of it. I thank God now that neither one of them listened to me. God has blessed me with a wonderful family. I have a loving, supporting wife who loves the Lord. I have a daughter who as a young teenager was closer to the Lord than most adults I knew. I did not realize that a child could love me that much. I love you, Michelle, and I am proud of you. I have in-laws that I would fight you over. Words cannot describe how much they mean to me. Jimmie and Shirley, you are the best! (Shirley has now gone on to be with the Lord and Jimmie has a lot of health issues and I'm even having a few as well but it has been good.) God will give you the best, if you will allow him. God wants to bless you with the best he has to offer. He is offering grain-fed beef, not a tough, poor, range cow; yet, some will not listen to God and end up eating briar goat instead.

God wants you to do more than just get by. He wants you to have an abundant life. Jesus said, "*I have come that they may have life and that they may have it more abundantly.*" (John 10:10) The word abundantly does not mean you will be rich monetarily. It means you will have a full life! God desires that you have an abundant life because he loves you, and so that you may be a channel of blessing to others. We are not to hoard all the blessings of God. Christians are to be the pipeline by which God's blessings flow.

The son in this parable had experienced a life without the father. He had come to appreciate the blessings of the father, more than those who had never been away from his presence. He realized how from the depths of sin he had come, and he never wanted to go back. He had been shod with the gospel, and he was making tracks all over the community, telling what the father had done for him. He had been changed forever. Instead of lustful desires, he had love for his fellowman. Instead of hoarding wealth, he wanted to share the gospel. Instead of attracting attention to himself, he desired to tell people about the grace of God. Instead of beating people down, he tried to lift them up. Instead of leading people astray, he tried to lead them to a path of righteousness. Before the son left home, he worked in drudgery. Now the son's heart was filled with love for the father, and his desire was to serve the father in any way that the father would allow him.

I am sure that the son in this parable must have had the same feelings I felt when I returned home. I had peace in my heart that I had never felt before. It was a peace that the Bible tells us about. *And the peace of God, which passeth all understanding, shall keep your hearts and minds through Christ Jesus.* (Phil. 4:7) There was joy in my heart that I could not explain. *Yet believing, ye rejoice with joy unspeakable, and full of glory.* (1 Peter 1:8) I desired to know the ways of the Lord. I had the feelings of the psalmist as he wrote, *"Show me your ways, o Lord; teach me your paths. Lead me in your truth and teach me, for you are the God of my salvation; on you I wait all the day."* (Ps. 25:4-5) Through the love of God, I had been given a desire to study the scriptures. I had never liked studying anything, except a good time, but now my interest and my attitude had changed. I began to prefer gospel music to country or rock. I had a genuine concern for others, even those that I did not particularly like. I had become calm under intense situations. I first thought it was because I had given up caffeine, but then I realized I could drink two or three cups of coffee and the calm feeling still remained. I found myself worrying less about my financial condition and more about those who had not come to know the saving grace of God through our Savior, Jesus Christ. Experiencing the love of God totally changed my life, and I wanted to tell the world about it. My desire was now to please the Father, not the world; after all, he gave his best for me. He gave his son!

Many people take for granted the blessings of God. Many times it is because they do not realize just what God has done for them. They still think that in some way, because of their goodness, they have a relationship with God. They believe that because they have read the Bible or can quote scripture that they have a home in heaven. The old saying, "It is not what you know, it is who you know that counts," could never be more true. I would rather know Jesus than to have a doctorate in Bible any day, because it is only through Jesus that you can have a relationship with the Father. *For there is no other name under heaven given among men by which we must be saved.* (Acts 4:12)

This relationship is available to you; all you have to do is ask. Call on the Lord with a repentant heart, trust Jesus as your Lord and Savior, submit to him, and ask him to take control of your life, and your eternity will be secure. *For whosoever shall call upon the name of the lord shall be saved.* (Rom. 10:13) Many people want to take this scripture out of context and think that whenever I'm in trouble I can call on Jesus like a cosmic Santa Claus or a Genie in a bottle. If I call on His name He will come and rescue me. The Biblical context is that justification comes by repentance; so when we call on the name of the Lord, we are calling with a repentant heart that has turned from our sin. This was not a flippant confession! During the time that Romans was written, Christians were being persecuted. They were experiencing hideous, torturous death for being a follower of Christ. They would be tied to poles, covered with tar, and lighted on fire to light the streets of Rome. Many who received spiritual life were being tortured and killed for it. Not many in our lifetime have been forced to die for their faith but all that has led to was weak faith. Most of us are only called to die to self; die to our selfish desires and to our self-righteousness. Unfortunately most professing Christians today can't even accomplish that. Pastors and Evangelist everywhere are trying to get more professions of faith when what we really need is more people submitting to Jesus! We need more of those who are willing to leave the past behind, press on, no matter the situation, or the persecution, and follow Christ. *I count not myself to have apprehended; but this one thing I do, forgetting those things which are behind, and reaching forth unto those things which are before, I press toward the mark for the prize of the high calling of God in Christ Jesus.* (Phil 3:13-14) Will you come along?

Chapter 11

Luke 15:25-26 Now his older son was in the field. And as he came and drew near to the house, he heard music and dancing. So he called one of the servants and asked what these things meant.

The older son had been a faithful son. He had done his best to do his father's wishes. This day was like any other for him. As he was returning from the daily chores, he heard all the commotion. Not knowing what had occurred while he was working, he questioned one of the servants as to what all of the racket was about.

This son represents certain professing Christians in the church body, those who have made a decision for Christ. They have been faithful to stay with the Father, and they go about doing the daily chores of the church. They may be deacons, teachers, committee chairmen, or just members who are continually supporting the church. They are good people who have never seemed to stray too far from the Lord. They have strived all their lives to walk the straight and narrow path of righteousness. These people are usually well respected in the area in which they live and are considered to be fine, upstanding citizens of the community.

The older son should be commended for his loyalty, because he never left his father's homeland. He was continually in a place of service for the father, and he took his jobs seriously. He is like the Christian who has taught Sunday school for years, who is always willing to take on the job when no one else will. He is like the deacon who is always in contact with his church members, checking on their needs and lending a hand whenever it is needed. He is like those on the grounds committee who keep the grass cut and the hedges trimmed. He is like the building committee member who is always looking for ways to improve and repair the Lord's house. He represents those who are committed to church attendance and are always in the father's house on Sundays and Wednesday nights. Many Christians are very committed to the church, just as the son in this parable was very committed to the father's homeland, but do they all understand the plan and will of the father?

It is God's desire that we remain faithful, but also that we carry our faith outside the parameters of the church walls and church grounds. It is God's desire that many of the lost come home, and he has a plan to bring them home. His plan is to involve other Christians in taking the gospel (the good news) to all those who have lost their way and have become entangled in the lures of the world. Jesus gave a command to all his followers. "*Go therefore and make disciples of all the nations, baptizing them in the name of the father and of the son and of the Holy Spirit.*" (Mat. 28:19) Jesus did not offer this as a suggestion. He did not say we should go if we feel like it or if we receive another revelation from the Father. Remember, Jesus has all the authority of the Father. *Jesus came and spoke to them saying, "All authority has been given to me in heaven and on earth.*" (Mat. 28:18) When Jesus says, "Go," it is straight from God himself. We are not to question God or make excuses. We should just go. Some may say that God has not told them to witness to others. If you are a disciple, a believer, a follower of Christ, then you have been told. God not only told you, he put it in writing in Matthew chapter 28, verses 19 and 20. Jesus did not say go and make contacts. Some say I will establish a relationship with someone so I can share Christ at a later date. That lame idea was taught in churches back in the 90's. Jesus didn't say, go and make friends; He said go and make disciples. Who are the hardest people to share the Gospel with? Your friends; because you tend to give them more grace than truth! Jesus told us to make disciples and from that group of disciples you will find your dearest friends. It has been said that you really don't choose your friends; your friends choose you. You are drawn to those who accept you as you are. If you share the Gospel with friends that you have accepted (as they are) or they have accepted you (as you are) they now must confront the sin in their lives and to accept the Gospel they must turn away from who they are. They also look at you as a person different than who they accepted. Certain scenarios usually follow. You may be tempted to compromise your relationship with Christ in order to maintain a friendly relationship with a worldly person. If you don't compromise, they will get mad and break friendship with you, usually running you down as well as the Gospel you represent, or they will tell you what you want to hear with no real change in their lives in order to continue to receive the benefits of associating with you. Either scenario ends with broken relationships, broken hearts, and no new disciples. Make a disciple and you will have a friend, because you have a connection, you have a bond; you have a mediator for any problem that may arise. That mediator is Jesus Christ! When Jesus is the mediator, all problems can be resolved. Do you want true friends, make disciples – true friendship will come.

Some professing Christians do not see the importance of the command to go and make disciples. They make the excuse that God only said that once or twice in the Bible, indicating that they do not think it is that important. That was a Proverbs 12:1

statement if I ever heard one. My dad would sometimes tell me something to do. If I didn't immediately start in that direction, he would not repeat himself. He would sometimes say, "I'm not going to tell you again". The interpretation of that south Georgia lingo is you better get started on what I told you or I have a belt that will help you pick up the pace; your choice! If we neglect the command of Christ which is a command from God, chastisement will follow! You may feel incapable, unsure, or afraid, but remember you will not be alone. Jesus Christ is with you. Jesus said, "*I am with you always, even to the end of the age.*" (Mat. 28:20)

Many Christians have the idea that their job is to keep everything running correctly inside the church walls or on the church grounds. They think if they erect an attractive church building and put up a sign, God will cause sinners to be drawn in. I have heard professing Christians speaking of the lost, say, "If they want to know the Lord, they know where the church is. They can come to us." That idea may sound logical, but it is not God's plan.

To know God's plan, we must seek God's word and follow the one in whom God has given all authority, Jesus Christ. Jesus came into this world not only to bring salvation to us but also to be a model for all Christians to follow. Jesus went to the synagogues and temples to worship, but he also spent time alone with God in prayer. *And in the morning, rising up a great while before day, he went out, and departed into a solitary place, and there prayed.* (Mark 1:35) If Jesus needed time alone with God in prayer, you can be sure that we need time alone in prayer also. Although Jesus was sinless, he did not disassociate himself from sinners. He constantly reached out to them, offering them a better life. *Now it happened, as he was dining in Levi's house, that many tax collectors and sinners also sat together with Jesus and his disciples; for there were many, and they followed him.* (Mark 2:15) There are many religious leaders today who act just as the religious leaders did in Jesus day. They will not lower themselves to associate with certain people, and they will ridicule anyone who does. They are quick to point out the sin in other people's lives, but fail to see their own shortcomings. One can never really know Christ without recognizing the sin in one's own life. The scribes and Pharisees spent their lives studying the word of God, yet they failed to recognize that Jesus was the one who spoke the very words of God, just as the Old Testament had prophesied. *I will raise up for them a prophet like you from among their brethren, and will put my words in his mouth, and he shall speak to them all that I command him.* (Deut. 18:15) When the scribes and Pharisees ridiculed Jesus for associating with sinners, Jesus replied, "*Those who are well have no need of a physician, but those who are sick. I did not come to call the righteous, but sinners, to repentance.*" (Mark 2:17) If the religious leaders of yesterday and today truly accepted the scriptures, they would realize that they, too, are in need of a Savior. *All we like sheep have gone astray; we have turned, every one, to his own way.* (Isaiah 53:6) Paul, the writer of Romans, explains it this way, "*There is none righteous, no, not one.*" (Rom. 3:10) When we fail to follow Christ's lead in reaching out to a lost and dying world, we find ourselves totally disobeying a command of God, to go and make disciples.

There was a story of a young boy who left the city to go and spend some time with his grandparents on the farm. About daylight the grandfather woke up the boy. They went out and gathered the eggs, fed the chickens and hogs. They milked the cow and put out some hay and cleaned out the barn stalls. Grandmother rang the bell in the front yard and they went back in the house for breakfast. As the young fellow was hurrying to finish his last few bites the grandfather slapped him on the back and said, "Come on son, it's time to go to work." The grandson said, "I thought was what we have been doing". The grandfather smiled and replied, "Anything that is done in the house, around the house, or for the house is chores. The work is done in the field." Many people are extremely proud of the work they do at church, and it is something that needs doing, but we must never forget – the work is done in the field. *Behold, I say to you, lift up your eyes and look at the fields, for they are already white for harvest!* (John 4:35)

Even though the older son in the parable could be commended for his loyalty, we begin to get a glimpse of a flaw in his character in Luke 15:26 when he asked the servants what these things meant. Though he had been loyal to the father, we begin to see that he did not really understand the nature of the father. He had always seen the father as the one who laid down the law, not as a loving father who wished to bless his children.

Many Christians today have the same problem. They are still struggling through life trying to live by the law, while God is offering them grace. They are working hard to please God by follow the Ten Commandments, but what God really wants is a relationship. A relationship with the Father is available through a relationship with his son, Jesus. The Ten Commandments cannot save you from an eternity in hell. The only thing that can is a relationship with Jesus Christ. Jesus said, "*No one comes to the father except through me.*" (John 14:6) The commandments were given so we would realize that we need that relationship with God.

Before you go any farther, maybe you should go back and read the last paragraph again to be sure you understand what is being said. There have been those who have said that I was running down the Ten Commandments. I personally believe that the Ten Commandments should be posted in every home, school, and building in the country. Again, let me say that God gave the Ten Commandments to show us our sin and bring us to the realization that we need a savior. I have heard little old ladies say, "I have lived by the ten commandments all my life." I hate to disappoint you, ladies, but you have not. The Bible says, "*All have sinned, and if we say that we have no sin, we deceive ourselves, and the truth is not in us."* (1 John 1:8) Ladies and gentlemen, we have all failed. We cannot say that we believe in the Bible and reject that fact. That is why Jesus came to this earth to pay the price for our sin. We have failed to keep the Ten Commandments, but if we fail to accept Jesus, we have failed to accept God's plan for our redemption. Jesus paid the price with his blood at Calvary. *In whom we have redemption through his blood, the forgiveness of sins, according to the riches of his grace.* (Eph. 1:7)

Are you still trying to follow the Ten Commandments, or are you following Christ? If you follow Jesus, you will not have to worry about the Ten Commandments because he will never lead you astray. If you are led by the spirit of God, you will not have to worry about the commandments of God because the spirit of God is the very nature of God. If you are led by the spirit of God, you will be living in the will of God, and God will be furnishing the power for you to succeed. Many professing Christians have never experienced this power that God provides to succeed. They never have found themselves in the position to see God's power at work. They have read in the Bible about it. They may have even heard others talk about their experiences seeing God at work, but they personally have never experienced it. Because they have personally never experienced it their faith is superficial or weak at best. They struggle to step out in faith to do what God is calling them to do, so they don't. Since they are not obedient to act on the leading of the Holy Spirit, they are now not in the position to see God work. Do you want your faith to grow? Do you want to see God do amazing and wondrous things? If so, follow the Holy Spirit as He attempts to lead you. Don't resist, step out in faith and obedience. You will find yourself with a front row seat to experience the wonderful works of God! The Holy Spirit is available to you this very moment. *Ask, and ye shall receive, that your joy may be full.*

(John 16:24) Following rules and regulations can be tiring. Follow Jesus through the power of the Holy Spirit, and you will find the true joy of Christian life. You will come to understand the nature of God and not just his laws.

God's nature is revealed in his word, but many professing Christians do not study God's word enough to find these truths. For some reason, they cannot get past the "thou shalt nots" in the Bible. Christianity is not a "thou shalt not" religion. It is a "go and do" relationship with our Lord and Savior, Jesus Christ.

Many claiming Christianity know the stories in the Bible. They know about Daniel in the lion's den and how David killed Goliath, but they fail to know the spiritual truths behind the stories. What adds to the problem are the untruths which have been taught from the pulpit. Most professing Christians do not study God's word enough to know when someone is in error, and they take whatever the preacher says as the gospel. Unfortunately, there are times when those in the pulpit let their opinions get in the way of the gospel. On a number of occasions, I have heard people who have been attending church regularly for sixty or seventy years quote something they say is in the Bible, but is not there. They explain a scripture totally wrong all because that is the way they heard it from the pulpit. I always encourage people to take their Bibles to church, follow along with the pastor or evangelist, so they may come to know the nature of the Father, and not the man behind the pulpit.

Do you know the nature of the Father, or are you like the older son in the parable? Are you attempting to follow the commandments or are you following Christ? Are you following Rules or are you resting in Jesus? Are you a disciple, or have you just made a decision? Do you have to ask one of the father's servants what it all means? It would be ashamed to live a lifetime of attempting to follow rules and miss the relationship. If you miss the relationship and continue a life of rule following it will result in one of two outcomes. You will be filled with pride like the elder son who thinks he has no sin or you will always worry that you may not be welcomed to the Father's house. Are you prideful or are you spending your life questioning every step you take, wondering if this step will send you tumbling into the pits of hell? If so, stop worrying and start trusting. Trust Jesus as your Lord and Savior, and trust that he has paid the price for you. Trust that Christ will make known the nature of God to you. Trust God to give you understanding of the scriptures. If you are having trouble with any of these things, ask God to help you. I guarantee you, he will. *Ask, and it will be given to you; seek and you will find; knock, and it will be opened to you.* (Mat. 7:7)

Chapter 12

Luke 15:27-28 And he said to him, "Your brother has come, and because he has received him safe and sound, your father has killed the fatted calf." But he was angry and would not go in. Therefore his father came out and pleaded with him.

The young son had returned home safely, the father was overjoyed, and he wanted to celebrate, so he killed the fatted calf to prepare for the party. He did not skimp on the preparations. He did not bring out baloney, potted meat, or sardines; he brought out the best. The safety of a father's child is important to him, just as the eternal safety of God's children is top priority with God. Just as the father in the parable sacrificed the best he had for the return of the younger son, so the father in heaven sacrificed the best he had when he sent his son to pay for our sins at Calvary.

As the servant explained what was happening inside, the Bible says, "The older son was angry." The anger was not a feeling that just happened. The Bible says, "He was angry." The anger and resentment that the older son felt had been with him for a while. He was angry because his younger brother received his inheritance early. He resented his brother for leaving home, and although he would not admit it, he probably felt bitter because he stayed behind.

You may be wondering why a Christian, someone who has been in the presence of the Father, would feel bitter for being there. There will be more light shed on this subject as we go along. As we look at the older son more closely, we might also ask, "How could a true Christian, one who knows God and is familiar with his ways through a relationship with Jesus Christ, be upset about someone coming back into the home?"

Just because a person attends church regularly, serves on a church committee, teaches Bible study, or serves as a deacon or even a pastor does not guarantee perfection. We would hope, but there is also no guarantee that they are eternally secure or that they have a relationship with the Father.

You might ask, "How someone could be a pastor, teach Bible study, or be a deacon without having a relationship with the Father?" The answer is simple. You can know about God and not know God. God may use people who do not have a personal relationship with him for the purpose of bringing others to know him. For example, Jesus sent out the twelve disciples. Jesus said, "*As you go, preach, saying, the kingdom of heaven is at hand.*" (Mat. 10:7) Jesus gave them authority to "*...heal the sick, cleanse the lepers, raise the dead, cast out demons.*" (Mat. 10:8) Later speaking of the twelve disciples, Jesus said, "*Did I not choose you, the twelve, and one of you is a devil?*" (John 6:70) *He spoke of Judas Iscariot; the son of Simon, for it was he who would betray him, being one of the twelve.* (John 6:71) All who are in the presence of the Father do not always belong to the Father. Judas Iscariot was in the presence of the Son of God, but from the scriptures it seems that he was a lost soul. Jesus spoke of him as being a devil, and the devil is not only lost, but also condemned. Speaking of Judas Iscariot, Jesus said, "*Woe to that man by whom the son of man is betrayed! It would have been good for that man if he had not been born.*" (Mat. 26:24)

There are some who belong to the Father, who have not grown in their faith, and may not understand the nature of the Father as they should. If one truly knows God or has some understanding of his nature, they would know that God's greatest desire is to have all mankind return to him. The Bible says, "*The Lord is longsuffering toward us, not willing that any should perish but that all should come to repentance.*" If heaven rejoices over a sinner returning home, should we not as Christians do the same? After all, we are Christians, followers of Christ. Should we not react in the same way as Christ would?

How would Christ react to a sinner, a prodigal son, returning home? There is a song in the old Broadman Hymnal that tells what Christ would do.

> Sinners Jesus will receive;
> Sound this word of grace to all,
> Who the heavenly pathway leave,
> All who linger all who fall.
> Sing it o'er and o'er again,
> Christ receiveth sinful men.
> Make the message clear and plain,
> Christ receiveth sinful men.

Christ receiveth sinful men; unfortunately, there are many professing Christians who will not. They fail to remember that they too were in the same class. The reason they cannot relate to sinners all goes back to the problem we discussed a few chapters earlier. They have categorized sin in such a fashion that they feel their sins are not as bad as the sins of others; therefore, in their minds they were never in the same class as the sinners they refuse to accept. This is a teaching of man, not of God. In God's eyes, sin is sin, and there are no degrees of sin as far as salvation and justification go.

You cannot be partially saved and God does not grade on the curve. He grades on the cross where even those sins that people think are few and small still had to be paid for.

If you have broken one commandment, you have broken the law, and are, therefore, a sinner in the eyes of God. *For whoever shall keep the whole law, and yet stumble in one point, he is guilty of all.* (James 2:10)

If we claim Christianity, and do not show forgiveness, we are only fooling ourselves. If we show no mercy toward others, we are walking a spider web over the pits of hell. We cannot expect mercy if we show no mercy. *For judgment is without mercy to the one who has shown no mercy.* (James 2:13) Since we have all sinned, we all need mercy. Many cry for justice. If we received justice, we would all spend the rest of eternity in hell, separated from God. I personally do not want justice. I want mercy and, therefore, I must be merciful.

Many of those who claim to know the Lord still cling to those feelings of anger and resentment. Not only are they in danger themselves, but they are also hurting the cause of Christ. Those feelings of anger and resentment do not come from God. They are in total opposition to the gifts given by the Holy Spirit.

What if the older son had met the younger son before he had reached home? What if he had been exposed to the anger and resentment of the older son before he experienced the love and forgiveness of the father? If so he might have turned away and spent the rest of his life sad, cold, empty, alone, and resentful toward all the family.

Many people who claim to be Christians are acting in the very same manner as the older son, and because of their attitude, there will be lost people who will never be made to feel welcome in God's house. As a prodigal starts on his journey home, all too often he is met at the property line of the home place by what he feels is a pious, holier-than-thou finger-pointer, who will tell the prodigal that he can never change.

I have personally heard the anger and hatred as it spewed from the mouths of professing Christians. Words and phrases such as *selfish, sorry trash* and *you will never change* are often used. It is sad, but the people making those derogatory statements really believe what they are saying when they tell someone that they will never change. They can honestly believe that statement because they, personally, have never changed. They have never been able to change those feelings of anger and resentment. If they continue to try and handle it on their own, they will fail. Only God can truly change a person, through the power of the Holy Spirit. *The things, which are impossible with men, are possible with God.* (Luke 18:28) God can replace the anger with peace and replace the resentment with joy if the angry, resentful person will recognize their faults, repent, and let God take control.

This type person usually thinks that they can handle any problem they have on their own. They believe that God helps those who help themselves, and they believe that statement is biblical. The Bible never said, "God helps those who help themselves." As a matter of fact, the Bible teaches the exact opposite. The Bible teaches that God helps us because we cannot help ourselves. Spiritually speaking, we cannot pull ourselves up by our own bootstraps. No matter how hard we try, no matter how much we improve ourselves, we can never reach the state of holiness and righteousness that God demands. It is only by the grace of God that we may enter into the presence of the Father. *For by grace are ye saved through faith; and that not of yourselves: it is the gift of God: not of works, lest any man should boast.* (Eph. 2:8-9) You are saved by grace, not your good works. You receive this grace only by faith in Jesus alone. It is not what we can do; it is what God has already done through his son Jesus Christ. Not blind faith, not weak faith, but faith that trusts the savior enough to follow Him!

I was helping a couple trail a deer they had shot while hunting on our place. It was way after dark and we had been following the trail for a while. We finally realized we were not going to be able to find the deer. When you're following a blood trail your eyes are always looking down. You can easily lose your bearings in the woods. When we gave up the search the guy with me pointed up ahead and said, "If we stay headed in this direction we will come out by the truck". I replied, "No, if you head in that direction you will go into miles of woods; we have to go to the left and back to get to the truck". He had to make a decision. Was he going to trust himself, or the one who owns the property? He followed me and we got back to the truck safely. Are you going to follow your own way and be lost, or are you going to follow Jesus, the one who created it all? *For by Him were all things created that are in heaven, and that are in earth visible and invisible, whether they be thrones, or dominions, or principalities, or powers; all things were created by Him and for Him: and He is before all things, and by Him all things consist.* (Col. 1:16-17)

When we sin, we turn against God and that is our fallen nature, our human nature. The *carnal mind is enmity against God.* (Rom. 8:7) The Greek word for carnal mind means human nature. When we follow our own nature we are an enemy of God, but it is God who reconciles us to him. *For if, when we were enemies, we were reconciled to God by the death of his son, much more, being reconciled, we shall be saved by his life.* (Rom. 5:10)

It was the anger that the older son harbored that caused all those thoughts and feelings. This anger caused more problems the longer it went unresolved. The older son probably thought his anger toward the younger son was justified, but the younger son had not sinned against him. He had sinned against the father. The father's forgiveness toward the young son was unmerited, just as the older son's anger toward the young son was also unmerited. We can now see the difference in the nature of the father and the nature of the older son. As Christians, we are to take on the nature of Christ, and it is that nature that we are to show. We now begin to see the sinful nature of the older son, yet he had not recognized or would not admit he had a problem.

Jesus Christ came to this world to fulfill the law. Jesus said, "*Do not think I came to destroy the law or the prophets. I did not come to destroy but to fulfill.*" (Mat. 5:17) Jesus gave us a true interpretation and understanding of the law or commandments of God. Jesus taught that our sinful acts were a result of the sin in our hearts and minds. The sin was committed before the act had begun. To explain this, Jesus said, "*You have heard that it was said to those of old, you shall not commit adultery.*" (Mat. 5:27) People tend to think of sin as the act itself. Jesus said, "*But I say to you that whoever looks at a woman to lust for her has already committed adultery with her in his heart.*" (Mat. 5:28) If we would control our sinful thoughts and desires, the sinful acts would never occur.

Jesus used another example of the sin being committed before the act when he said, "*You have heard that it was said to those of old, you shall not murder, and whoever murders will be in danger of the judgment.*" (Mat. 5:21) People may be feeling the guilt of sin in their lives, but try and justify themselves by saying, "I have never killed anybody." Jesus said, "*But I say to you that whoever is angry with his brother without a cause shall be in danger of the judgment.*" (Mat. 5:22)

In this parable, the Bible tells us that the older son was angry and would not go in. The sin had already been committed, and there was no sign of repentance or remorse on his part. Although the son had never left the presence of the father and had seemed outwardly to be doing the will of the father, he was in total rebellion inside.

The older son was just like the religious people throughout the ages and those of today. Jesus warned those who seemed so religious in his day when he said, "*Woe to you, scribes and Pharisees, hypocrites! For you are like whitewashed tombs which indeed appear beautiful outwardly, but inside you are full of dead men's bones and all uncleanness.*" (Mat. 23:27) The Scribes and Pharisees were just like many people claiming to be Christians today who attend church regularly and appear to be living Christian lives outwardly but are full of anger and hatred. They are not really Christians at all, and as God's word tells us in Matthew 5:22, "*…are in danger of judgment.*"

If you have anger, resentment, or hatred in your heart that you are clinging to, you are in danger. Those are not qualities of a Christian. You may never admit it, and you may hide it from many in the community, but you can never hide it from God. God can see right into your heart and soul. There are two sinners in this parable. The younger son had been forgiven, but the father was still pleading with the other. *Therefore his father came out and pleaded with him.* (Luke 15:28) Are you harboring anger, hatred, or resentment in your heart toward someone? You may be keeping someone from entering the kingdom of heaven because of your attitude. As Christians we are to take on the nature of Christ, which is the nature of God. In the parable the Father that represents God has accepted the repentant young son home and is pleading with the older son to come in; basically to *enter into the joy of your Lord.* (Mat. 25:23) Instead of ridiculing or belittling those who are lost, shouldn't we be pleading as well! As Christians, that should be our new nature. Our old nature is a sinful nature and it may keep others from coming in. Your sin may also keep you out; you cannot hide from God. Stop a minute and honestly think about yourself.

God may be pleading with you this very moment. Turn from these thoughts and feelings and ask the Father for his help to change you, so that you may enter God's house with him.

Chapter 13

Luke 15:29 –30 So he answered and said to his father, "Lo, these many years I have been serving you; I never transgressed your commandment at any time; and yet you never gave me a young goat, that I might make merry with my friends. But as soon as this son of yours came, who has devoured your livelihood with harlots; you killed the fatted calf for him."

I grew up in a loving, honest, God-fearing family. My parents did the best they could to raise me in a way that the Bible teaches. *Foolishness is bound up in the heart of a child; the rod of correction will drive it far from him.* (Prov. 22:13) My parents certainly did not want a foolish child, and on occasion, they had to drive some foolishness away from me. My parents wanted me to grow up wise. *The rod and rebuke give wisdom, but a child left to himself brings shame to his mother.* (Prov. 29:15) I was not despised or hated by my parents. I was nurtured and loved, but I was also corrected and disciplined. *He who spares the rod hates his son, but he who loves him disciplines him promptly.* (Prov. 13:24) Of course, in my day we were more sophisticated than in Bible times; instead of rods, we use belts and switches. Nothing will get your attention like the sound of a leather belt sliding swiftly through belt loops. My dad could clear leather faster than Wyatt Earp and was always on target, even if the target was moving and it usually was. As I look back over my life, I must say that I deserved each and every whipping I received, except maybe one. I suppose, when you consider all the times I did need one and did not get it, I really came out ahead.

To prevent willful rebellion, pain is very much a part of corrective discipline. When we are young, attempting some stupid trick on our bicycles, we skin our knees, ears, and rears. It is then we learn there are some things that it is best we not attempt. It is better to spank a child to prevent him from playing out in the road than to allow him to be run over by a truck. Some will spout some skewed statistic and say spanking will not aid in correcting a child. If done correctly and Biblically it will not only aid in correction but aid in building character. Discipline should always be done for correction for rebellion and disobedience; never expressing a parents anger. Believe me, if done correctly, the board of correction to the seat of the problem will definitely prevent reoccurrences. When it is applied swiftly and decisively, it can also prevent reapplications in the near future. When it is applied correctly, it is like the old Bril Cream commercials used to say, "A little dab will do ya."

The older son in this parable may not have experienced many whippings. The son himself said, "I never transgressed your commandment at any time." He probably had never shown any outward sign of rebellion; therefore, he never needed any outward correction. His outward appearance was squeaky clean, but inside his heart lay the stains of sin. He was so concerned with keeping a clean public appearance that he failed to search the dark spots of his heart to see if those spots were shadows or filth.

Jesus warned the religious leaders in his day of making a clean outward appearance, while not being concerned about the filth within. *Woe to you, scribes and Pharisees, hypocrites! For you cleanse the outside of the cup and dish, but inside they are full of extortion and self-indulgence.* (Mat. 23:25) Jesus was instructing them to cleanse themselves on the inside and the outside could then be clean. *Blind Pharisee; first cleanse the inside of the cup and dish that the outside of them may be clean also.* (Mat. 23:26)

The cup and the dish represented the scribes and Pharisees themselves. The cup that would represent the older son in this parable might not have been full of extortion or self-indulgence, but it was full of resentment and selfishness. He resented that the younger son had been forgiven and did not want to share any of his father's possessions that remained. In his mind, all that remained of his father's estate should have belonged to him, and even though he had not yet taken possession of it, he had no intention of sharing any of it with his wayward brother. His resentment was so strong that he did not even refer to him as his brother when talking to his father, but rather as "that son of yours".

No matter how clean the outside may appear, it is the purity of the heart that makes one holy before God. *A good man out of the good treasure of his heart brings forth good; and an evil man out of the evil treasure of his heart brings forth evil.* (Luke 6:44) When you boil it all down, the heart of the matter is this: It is a matter of the heart! As the good or evil wells up inside of man, it will reveal itself first through words, then through deeds. *For out of the abundance of the heart his mouth speaks.* (Luke 6:44) Man may repress his evil deeds for a time, but the evil words are much harder to hide, for the first place evil will manifest itself is through the tongue. *But no man can tame the tongue. It is an unruly evil, full of deadly poison.* (James 3:8) One way to determine the righteousness of man is his ability to control his tongue. *If anyone does not stumble in word, he is a perfect man, able also to bridle the whole body.* (James 3:2)

We see the evil in the heart of the older son begin to manifest itself through his speech. He accused the father of showing partiality to the younger son by killing the fatted calf. He accused the father of never giving him anything for his years of service to him. The older son refused to stand on level ground with his younger brother. He felt he was better than he and, therefore, should be above him.

Some professing Christians also seem to think higher of themselves than others. Just as the older son claimed no relation to the younger son, many Christians cannot forgive or forget the past sins of other Christians. It seems some people feel that by constantly reminding others of their failures, it makes them look better. The Bible warns us of this type of thinking. *For whoever exalts himself will be humbled, and he who humbles himself will be exalted.* (Luke 14:11) We cannot lift ourselves or exalt ourselves. Only God can lift us up, and we certainly cannot lift ourselves up by putting someone else down. We should lift one another up and reach out to those in need. If we help others, we help Christ. *And the king will answer and say to them, "Assuredly, I say to you inasmuch as you did it to one of the least of these my brethren, you did it to me.* (Mat. 25:40)

We all stand on the same ground. We are all at the foot of the cross. None of us are worthy to be the supreme sacrifice for the sin of the world, for we are all sinners. We humans have a hard time confessing the fact that we are sinners. That is why we should follow Jesus not humans. We always want to put a "but" on the end of our confession. I may have sinned, but it was his fault, her fault, their fault, or the devil's fault, and if there is no one else to blame, it is God's fault for making me this way.

The human species has not changed at all since creation. Remember Adam's response as God confronted him about his sin in the Garden of Eden. *Then the man said, "The woman whom you gave to be with me, she gave me of the tree, and I ate."* (Gen. 3:12) First the man blamed the woman. "She gave it to me, God." It was her fault. Then man blamed God. "You gave her to me, God." This could be your fault. Before you ladies start to point your fingers, you had better read the next verse. When the woman was confronted, *"The woman said, 'The serpent deceived me, and I ate.'"* (Gen. 3:13) The woman said, "The devil made me do it." I bet you thought a twentieth century comedian made up that line. No, I am afraid it is as old as humanity, which is not quite as old as dirt. While we are on the subject of dirt, you did not crawl up out of the sea, like the evolutionists say. You were formed from the dirt and all the elements in your body can be found in the dirt. *And the lord God formed man of the dust of the ground, and breathed into his nostrils the breath of life; and man become a living being.* (Gen. 2:7)

I have often wondered what a difference it would have made in this world if, instead of making excuses, Adam and Eve would have fallen prostrate before God, admitted their sin, and begged for his forgiveness. They did not, and the sin of pride overtook them, as they were too proud to accept total responsibility for their actions. All sin puts a barrier between God and us. This barrier is an obstacle that prevents fellowship in God's grace. Pride is the last barrier, the last obstacle, which we have to break through to receive the grace God desires to offer us. It happened in the Garden of Eden, and it still happens today. Only confession and repentance can remove the barrier and bring us back into fellowship with God. There is <u>no obstacle</u> to God's grace that cannot be removed by confession and repentance!

Because of the older son's sin of pride, there was a barrier between the father and the son. He attempted to lay blame on the father and the younger son, while never addressing his own problems. In doing so, the older son missed the fellowship with the family and with the father.

The older son in the parable was acting much in the same way as Adam and Eve in the garden. Not only did the son not admit his sin, but he also tried to cover it up. Just as Adam and Eve sowed fig leaves together to cover themselves, the older son made an outward showing of obedience to cover the sin in his heart. Will we ever learn we cannot hide our sin from God? *O God you know my foolishness; and my sins are not hidden from you.* (Ps. 69:5)

When I was in college, there was one fellow who stood out from all the other guys on campus. We will call him Big John. I will not use his real name because what I am about to relate to you is mostly hearsay, but it does make a good point. I really do not know what his stats were, but he must have been about six foot, eight inches tall, or more, and his weight was probably over 400 pounds. Whatever his figures were, he was one big boy. You could always tell when John was in the group because he towered over the crowd. One day a group got together to carry out the latest fad on campus. (It was something I never got into, I might add.) I am sure you have heard about it—streaking, otherwise known as running naked. Streakers would usually have nothing on but their tennis shoes (you don't want stickers in your feet slowing you down) and a head covering of some kind to hide their identity. Running naked in public was frowned upon not only by the faculty and campus security but also by the city law enforcement officers. As the group of twenty-five or so students, with shirts covering their heads, rounded the corner by the humanities building, no matter how hard he tried to hide, everyone knew who was right in the middle of the pack. There went Big John! Did you know that no matter how good you think you have covered your sin, God can pick you out of a world of people easier than the student body could pick out Big John in a group of streakers? And, believe me, that was no problem at all.

We think we can hide our sins from God and man, and more times than not, we do not successfully hide them from either. People may not always confront you about your sin, although many times they know. God does confront us by bringing conviction upon your heart. When conviction comes, many times the person under conviction will lash out at someone around them, accusing them just as the older son accused the father and the younger son. I have seen many pastors, evangelists, teachers, and church members become hurt because of accusations from someone under conviction. I have heard people say that they are being condemned, talked down to, or preached down to, when that was not the intention at all. Years ago I preached a revival at a small country church. About a week later, my wife was in a conversation on the phone when the operator broke in and said there was an emergency call for me. I was in the shower so I immediately stepped out of the shower, wrapped a towel around me and stepped out in the hall. There was a lady on the line that was terribly distraught. She was crying and hysterical. I could hardly make out what she was saying. I tried to calm her and I ask her who she was. She never told me her name. She just kept saying, "You know who I am; you were preaching right at me last week". By the time the conversation was over, she had still never told me her name but I was completely dry. If you feel you are under condemnation from another Christian, before you lash out, make sure you are not mistaking conviction for condemnation. God may be trying to tell you something. Please listen.

It must be somewhat pitiful, but somewhat humorous, for the one who knows all, sees all, and hears all, to watch as we try to conceal our sin. Do not conceal it. Confess it and enter into the fellowship with the father and the family. I guarantee you will be much happier on the inside of God's house, having fellowship with the family, than standing on the outside, holding on to your resentment and anger. You need to get rid of whatever it is that is keeping you from fellowship with your Christian family. Whether it is anger, resentment, hatred, a bad attitude, or lack of forgiveness, it will all prevent you from having the relationship that God wants you to have with him and his family. Swallow your pride and come back into fellowship with the family. This is one time you will never hear the devil say, "Try it. You'll like it," because he knows you will, and your happiness in certainly not in his plan. Are you experiencing God's grace, or are you standing on the outside holding on to your bitterness, resentment, and anger? Remove these obstacles to God's grace, repent, let all those things go and listen as God says, "*Well done, my good and faithful servant; you were faithful over a few things, I will make you ruler over many things. Enter into the joy of your Lord.*" (Mat. 25:21)

Chapter 14

LUKE 15:31 AND HE SAID TO HIM, "SON, YOU ARE ALWAYS WITH ME, AND ALL THAT I HAVE IS YOURS."

The father told the son that everything he had was his. He reaffirmed the fact that he had brought the son into this world and everything he had was at the son's disposal. Of course, the father may have had some stipulations. The father would not have allowed his son to have a big "tho-down" as we used to call it where everyone was drunk and disorderly (though not all tho-downs are drunk and disorderly parties.) There were certain limitations, but the older son could have had a party for his friends anytime he desired. All of the father's servants, all of the father's possessions, and all of the father's influence were available to the son, but the son never took advantage of the benefits or the opportunities he had.

Just as the elder son had his father's servants available to him, we as Christians have God's servants helping us, even when we are not aware of it. *For he has given his angels charge over you, to keep you in all your ways.* (Ps. 91:11) God's angels are constantly about us. There are many times each day that these heavenly creatures protect us from harm, though we may not realize it. According to Dr. Billy Graham, we must have at least two guardian angels to protect us because of the plural form of *angels* in the text. God's servants are not here to do our wishes, but are here to do God's will, and God's will for us is better for us than our wishes.

We not only have the heavenly angels to help us in our time of need, we also have other Christians. When we become Christians, we also become servants of Christ, and, therefore, servants of mankind. What better way to show the love of Christ than to help one another? The apostle Paul certainly understood and taught this because he wrote, "*For though I am free from all men, I have made myself a servant to all, that I might win the more.*" (1Cor. 9:19)

We also have another helper that God has provided to lead and guide us in the right direction. God provided this helper after Christ ascended back into heaven. *And I will pray the father, and he will give you another helper, that he may abide with you forever.* (John 14:16) The helper in this passage is known as Holy Spirit. In the King James Version of the Bible he is referred to as a comforter. In the original Greek language, the word is *parakletos*, pronounced *par-ak-lay-tos*, which means an intercessor, consoler, advocate, and comforter. When we have fear in our lives brought on by earthly circumstances, it is not from God. *For God has not given us a spirit of fear, but of power and of love and of a sound mind.* (2 Tim. 1:7) Through the guidance of the Holy Spirit, we can obtain peace in our lives. The Bible tells us that this peace is beyond our comprehension. *And the peace of God, which surpasses all understanding, will guard your hearts and minds through Christ Jesus.* (Phil. 4:7) The Holy Spirit intercedes to God on our behalf when we do not even know what we should pray for. *Likewise the spirit also helps in our weaknesses. For we do not know what we should pray for as we ought, but the spirit himself makes intercession for us with groanings which cannot be uttered.* (Rom. 8:26)

The Holy Spirit does more than just comfort and intercede. He brings conviction upon us about our sin. *And when he has come, he will convict the world of sin, and of righteousness, and of judgment.*

(John 16:8) If there were no conviction about our sin, there would never be any repentance. The conviction we feel is sometimes a bad dose to swallow, but the sweetness of forgiveness is worth it all.

When heartfelt confession of our faith in Jesus Christ is made, the Holy Spirit then indwells the believer. *That good thing which was committed to you, keep by the Holy Spirit who dwells in us.* (1Tim. 1:14) When the Holy Spirit indwells us, he will instantly bring conviction upon us when we sin so that we may repent and keep ourselves in a right relationship with God. Since the Holy Spirit indwells, he is always available to us to teach us. *But the helper, the Holy Spirit, whom the father will send in my name, he will teach you all things and bring to your remembrance all things that I said to you.* (John 14:26) The spirit will guide us, just as he guided the disciples in New Testament history. Today, we have God's written word, and in order for the spirit to remind us of what Jesus said, we must have read what Jesus said. That is why it is so important for us to spend time reading God's word. When we face problems in our everyday lives, the Holy Spirit brings scripture to our remembrance that will allow us to know God's will in each and every situation.

The Holy Spirit protects us. *For I know that this will turn out for my deliverance through your prayer and the supply of the spirit of Jesus Christ.* (Phil. 1:19) The spirit transforms us by changing our attitude. *Now may the God of hope fill you with all joy and peace in believing, that you may abound in hope by the power of the Holy Spirit.* (Rom. 15:13) The Holy Spirit also gives us power to do what God expects from us. *But you shall receive power when the Holy Spirit has come upon you.* (Acts 1:8) All these things the Holy Spirit can and will do for us if we submit and do not resist him. *Do not quench the spirit.* (1Thes. 5:19)

One would think that with all this help available we would become strong in our faith and grow in knowledge of God.

Unfortunately, we, like the elder son in the parable, tend to become less dependent on the father when all our needs are being met. We think we have everything under control, and we just have no immediate need for God right now. What we fail to realize is that it is God who has everything under control, and we need to draw closer to him each and every day. The old hymn says it best:

> I need thee, O, I need thee,
> Every hour I need thee.
> O bless me now my savior,
> I come to thee.

During his last days, maybe even weeks or months, before the younger son left his dwelling place with the hogs, I am sure he spent many hours meditating on the things his father had said. All the instruction, all the warnings, all the concerns, and all the love that the father had shown him were constantly on his mind. It was the meditation on his father's words that brought sorrow for his actions and a change in his direction. If we, as Christians, spend time meditating on God's word, we too will become sorrowful for our actions and will repent and change our direction.

Years ago I was mentoring a fellow who was young in the faith. I told him that the longer I walked with God and the more I studied His word the more sinful I realize I am and the more I realize how little I know. Years later he confessed that when I said that to him, he thought that was the dumbest statement he had ever heard. He now will tell you, he knows exactly what I meant! Meditate on God's word! It will help you to understand just how much you need a savior!

The elder son, because of his presence before the father and because there was no trouble in his life and his needs were being met, probably spent less time meditating on the words of the father.

Although he was present with the father and working for the father, his mind was not on his father's will because he was not spending time meditating on his father's words. Many in the modern church are working for the father and no one is impressed watching people work. After all, who wants another job? Christians should be submitting to the Father's will and allowing the Father to work through them. By submitting to the leading of the Holy Spirit you will be able to accomplish things far beyond your natural ability, and that is impressive!

There are many Christians today who are in the presence of God, doing the work of God, and attending God's house every Sunday, but it has become a ritual for them. There is no feeling in their worship. They are just going through the motions, and all too often, there is no true worship at all. If you ask many people how they worship, they will respond by saying, "We go to church, we sing songs, and we listen to the preacher." These things in themselves are not worship. They are only the means by which we may obtain a worshipful atmosphere. Until you can become oblivious to all that is around you and concentrate solely on God by allowing him to speak to your heart, you have not experienced true worship. The problem lies in not spending time meditating on God's word. A person would eventually starve to death if he ate only one meal a week, yet many people only feast off of God's word once or twice a week. Without even realizing it, they are spiritually starving to death, and spiritual death is not an end. It is an eternity separated from God. Without spending time in and on God's word, you cannot know the will of God nor can you "*...be transformed by the renewing of your mind.*" (Rom. 12:2) When your mind has been renewed, "*You may prove what is that good and acceptable and perfect will of God.*" (Rom. 12:2) God's will and God's desire is for "*...all men to be saved and to come to the knowledge of the truth.*" (1 Tim. 2:4) If God's will has become your will, then you too will desire all to be saved, and the fruit of the spirit will be shown through your life. You will then become an encourager instead of a ridiculer. (*Kindness and Goodness*) You will be able to override the feelings of resentment of the natural fallen man and gently welcome those who are coming out of sin into the family of God. (*Gentleness and Self-control*) You will have (*Peace and Joy*) about you, so others will be drawn to you. You will be able to overlook and forgive the shortcomings of others. *(Longsuffering)* All this can be done because you have the (Love) of God in you. In this way, the fruits of the spirit of God will be manifest in you. (Gal. 5:22-23)

The elder son in this parable could be described as a religious person, but he lacked spirituality. I had an aunt who lived to be over 100 years old. She was a very religious person. When she was able, she was very active in her church; she was present at all the functions. Often she would give a lengthy discourse to someone about the sin in their life. She would point her finger, and the "thou shalt nots" would flow. I found myself on the opposite end of her finger on many occasions. She spent her last several years in the nursing home and her last year totally confined to the bed. During that time, I saw an amazing change take place in her life. She had more time to meditate on God's word. She spent more time in prayer, praying continually for her family. Her greatest desire was for all her family to come to know Jesus Christ as their Lord and Savior. She grew closer to God, and the fruit of the spirit began to manifest in her speech. I was blessed to watch as she was transformed from a religious person into a spiritual person.

Many elderly people find their health failing, and wonder why God would leave them in this world without the ability to take care of themselves? It could be that they too have not taken advantage of the things that God has made available to them. Maybe they have been in the presence of God for years, as the elder son in the parable, but still do not understand the ways of God as expressed through his son, Jesus Christ. Much of their knowledge of God has come from Hollywood movies and second hand information from people who don't know anymore about God than they do, instead of getting their information from the original source. God may be giving them this time, when other things in life will not distract them, in order for them to come to know Him better instead of knowing man's teaching. *That we should no longer be children, tossed to and fro and carried about with every wind of doctrine, by the trickery of men.* (Eph. 4:14) There may be some part of their spiritual life in which they need to be matured by learning the truths of God so they may speak the truth and share the gospel with those around them. *But, speaking the truth in love may grow up in all things into him who is the head - Christ.* (Eph. 4:15) They may need to meditate on God's word because God wants them to know him better, and through this knowledge they just might find that there is still a job for them to do. It might be that they have family and friends who desperately need prayer, and God is now providing the time for them to do just that. Pray!

There are many people in churches today who are just like the elder son in this parable. They have been in church all their lives yet have still not taken advantage of all God has to offer as our heavenly Father. They continue to try and live their Christian lives in their own ability while God is standing by with all the resources in the universe, and they do not know God or trust him enough to realize that his desire is to provide for them.

All that we attempt to do as Christians should be done through the power of the Holy Spirit that God provides. We should never depend on our own strength to accomplish God's work. We should be as the apostle Paul and depend totally on the power available through God, so that men's faith will not be in human wisdom, but in the power of God. *I was with you in weakness, in fear, and in much trembling. And my speech and my preaching were not with persuasive words of human wisdom, but in demonstration of the spirit and of power, that your faith should not be in the wisdom of men but in the power of God.* (1 Cor. 2:3-5) When we try to do God's work under our own power, we are only showing "*...a form of Godliness but denying the power thereof.*" *(2* Tim. 3:5*)* The last part of the verse in 2 Timothy 3:5 is translated somewhat differently in the different translations of the Bible, but they are all true. The King James Version says, " *...from such turn away,*" meaning we should turn away from those who act in such a manner. The New International Version reads, "*having nothing to do with them,*" which is interpreted the same way. The New King James Version reads, "*...and from such people turn away.*" This version could indicate that people do turn away from those who have a form of godliness but deny God's power. Although the reading is different, it is still true. Those who go through the ritual of religion and never have the power of God expressed through their lives will turn off people who are in need of a savior. To them, it is just another dead church. It is not the lives of others that draw people to Jesus Christ, but the power of God revealed through those lives that people desire to see.

Are you using all that is available to you from your heavenly Father? If the power of God is not working through your life, then your answer must be "no" to the previous question. What are you waiting for? The promise and provision for the availability of God's power has been made and fulfilled. Jesus made the promise. *You shall receive power when the Holy Spirit has come upon you.* (Acts 1:8) The provision was made at Pentecost after Jesus ascended into heaven, and it is available to you today. You can have the power to live and accomplish things that are above and beyond your personal ability. It is really a matter of trust. Do you trust God for your salvation? Why not trust him for your provision? You may say that you believe it, but you do not have that power. God's word tells us what to do. Jesus said, *"Ask and you will receive, that your joy may be full."* (John 16:24) You may say, "I have asked but I don't feel the power". It is not about feelings, it is about faith! Walk in it! You will never know what God can do through you until you step out in faith no matter how you feel. It will not be you working but the Lord working through you! Stop trying to work for God and trust that He can and will work through you. The words Jesus spoke to the apostle Paul are just as real for you today. *My grace is sufficient for you, for My strength is made perfect in weakness.* (2Cor. 12:9) What are you waiting for?

Chapter 15

Luke 15:32 It was right that we should make merry and be glad, for your brother was dead and is alive again, and was lost and is found.

The father was elated at the return of his son because he had missed his presence and his fellowship. The father told his older son that they all should be happy over the return of his younger brother. His homecoming should have been a joyous occasion, just as there is joy in heaven over one who repents and turns to the Lord. *Likewise, I say to you, there is joy in the presence of the angels of God over one sinner who repents.* (Luke 15:10)

Many of us may never experience the feeling of loss this father must have felt while his son was away. The closest feeling to this that many of us will feel is dropping off that little five or six year old at the school house for the first time. (Unless you've been there you won't understand the correlation.) My wife cried for two weeks when our daughter started to school. Even I had no comprehension of what my wife was going through until the morning I took my daughter to meet the bus. She was so little. She looked so helpless surrounded by all these huge kids. It made me want to run and grab her up in my arms and take her back to the safety of our own home. My dad has said that the hardest time he had was when he drove me to the college campus, dropped me off, and left me there.

At the time of the 1st writing of this book I had not gotten to that point in life but is was drawing very near; now my grandson is drawing near to college age.

Unless your son has gone to war in some foreign land, with no word from him in months, or unless you are a parent of a child that has been abducted, you cannot even imagine the emotional stress this father was going through. He may not have known whether his son was dead or alive. Without communication from the son, the father feared the worst, but always hoped that one day he would see his son again. It was an answer to the father's many prayers to see the son walking up the road on his way home. It was certainly a time for joy and celebration.

When a person comes to know Jesus as their Lord and Savior, it too should be a time of joy and celebration. It seems that in our churches today our joy of someone coming to Christ has been lost. Instead of a joyous celebration, it seems more like a somber ritual. They walk the aisle; there is a motion to accept, then a second, and a vote to accept. We then line up like zombies, walk down the aisle, shake hands, and say, "Glad to have you," or "You are one of us now." We should take a good look at ourselves before we use that last line, because sometimes that may not be very encouraging. After hearing that statement, it is a wonder some young Christians do not scream and run out of the church never to return again. Why is there no joyous celebration? Is the problem our lack of concern for the lost? Are we that far away from God's plan and God's vision?

There has been one time in my life that I have seen a church truly joyous over a soul being saved. I had been visiting Christian Life Church in Eufaula, Alabama, when they had revivals and special events. Pastor Ken Jackson believed in revival being a continual event, not just for four nights. I pray that he never changes. He had arranged for evangelist Andy Bryan to come and lead the worship services two nights each month. This went on for two years.

People were being saved, and lives were being changed. There was one young lady that always asked the church to pray for her husband to receive Christ, and they did every month for two years. I am sure that they were praying even more than that. Pam was praying continually. This was truly a praying church. Some of the most power-filled prayer I have ever experienced has been there at the altar of Christian Life Church. I have witnessed as people were healed, lives were changed, and souls were saved. After two years of praying for Pam's husband, he came to church and walked the aisle to receive Christ as his Savior. Before he had gotten half way down to the altar, the whole church began yelling, "Praise God!" and "Hallelujah!" People began hugging one another, hands were clapping, and tears were flowing. This event had been a prayer of this church for two years that I knew of. Their prayers were answered; they were elated, and they praised God for it. Oh, if we were all that excited and joyful when a soul was saved or a wandering child of God came home! Think how happy our heavenly father would be of us and with us. We should be joyful because it is the right thing to do.

I have heard many messages on these scriptures about the prodigal son, and over the years this story has been taught in Sunday school many times. We all concentrate on the younger son returning home from a wayward life of sin. We talk about God's grace and God's forgiveness toward the younger son, but there is one thing that over the years no one has ever mentioned. What happened to the elder son? The scriptures leave him outside the house of the father. We are not told the response of the elder son to the father's pleas to come in and join the celebration. We are only told in Luke 15:28 that he was angry and would not come in. He had come to the door of the father's house and had refused to enter. Did he let his pride, jealousy, and his hard heartedness toward his younger brother keep him out of the father's house? What about you? Will pride keep you out of the father's house in heaven? Will you spend your life on earth close to the kingdom only to come to the gates of heaven and refuse to enter?

Those who will never enter heaven because of pride have ridiculed many people for the sin and mistakes in their life. Getting people saved from an eternity in hell is really not that hard; getting people to realize that is where they are headed is. They think that because they are members of a church and were raised in church and because their parents were church members that they will automatically be allowed in heaven. They say they believe in Jesus Christ, but their belief has not affected their attitudes or decisions in their life. Jesus said, "*Let your light so shine before men, that they may see your good works and glorify your father in heaven.*" (Mat. 5:16) Our lights should reflect good works and not pride, jealousy, bitterness, and unforgiveness. These do not describe a person through which the Holy Spirit is working. When there is no evidence of the Holy Spirit working, it makes one wonder if the Holy Spirit is even present. If the Holy Spirit is not present, that person is headed in the wrong direction no matter how long he or she has been a member of the church. I had rather be two hundred miles away, headed toward heaven, than to be three feet from heaven headed away from it. The direction you are headed when you breathe your last breath may determine your destination.

It is hard to imagine that one could come so close to heaven yet not enter. A scribe came to Jesus and questioned him about the scriptures. The scribe agreed with the answers Jesus gave and Jesus replied to him, "*You are not far from the kingdom of God.*" (Mark 12:34) A person can know all the right answers, be close to the kingdom, but still miss it. Without Jesus Christ in your life and in your heart, you too will miss the kingdom.

If Jesus resides in your heart, there is no room for pride. Does the sin of pride keep you from worshiping with people from different social classes or different races? I have heard people say of someone of a different race, "If he is really saved, he will want to worship with his own kind." I have news for you. If you are a born again child of God and he is a born again child of God, then you are his own kind. In God's eyes, there are only two kinds of people, those who have accepted Jesus as their Lord and Savior (God's children), and those who have not (the devil's children). Jesus crossed all social and racial barriers to minister to people. Should we not follow the lead of our Lord and Savior? If you refuse to cross racial and social barriers to minister to people, then I suggest you refrain from singing the next time the music minister leads the congregation in the song, "Footsteps of Jesus." Do not sing it if you really do not believe it.

> (Chorus) Footprints of Jesus that make the
> pathway glow,
> We will follow the steps of Jesus, where'er they go.
>
> (3rd verse) If they lead through the temple holy,
> preaching the word,
> Or in the homes of the poor and lowly,
> serving the Lord.

Many will say they are willing to reach across racial and social barriers until the ministry begins; then they disappear. We have a small country church but over the years we have done a lot of ministry. At maximum we had about 45 attending. We would hold a Bible school every year for approximately 50 to 60 kids. They were from broken homes, single parent homes, homes that the front door was not even on the hinges. They were from neighborhoods where drug abuse, and child abuse was plentiful. Many nights at 9:30 we were riding around town trying to find a place to drop off kids because the mother wasn't home. We would go to grandma's house and she wasn't home so we would eventually drop them off at their aunt's house. There were times when 3 other local churches with a combined membership of 300 would go together to hold Bible school for about 60 to 80 kids, but most of those were not from the same neighborhood that we ministered to. Most of the kids we dealt with had 2 strikes against them; the 3rd pitch was on the way and it was a fast slider! A number of our group wondered if we had more time with them, could we make a difference. After several discussions, I told our church to be praying that a door would open if God wanted us to minister to these kids on a regular basis. Everyone seemed to be in agreement! After about 2 years God opened the door for us to work with the kids every week. We would pick them up after school, bring them out to Clay Hill, feed them supper, allow a little play time, (if you could call it that – it usually consisted of the adults breaking up fights) and then breaking up into age groups for Bible Study. It took about 6 months of meetings before we could get them out of the city limits before some kid was bloodying the nose of another! When we started this ministry we had about 45 attending our church. Within the first month we were ministering to about 45 kids each week and there would be a small group that would come on Sunday. Within three months our membership had dropped to 20 and by six months we were down to 17. We were down to a small group and it was almost more than we could handle. There were many nights we all felt like throwing in the towel, but I reminded them that we had prayed for this. Be careful what you pray for! It got worse. We were now down to about nine adults working with the kids each week. Fortunately, our numbers of kids dropped as well. We were now down to about 25 kids. It was a hard ministry. Our church family had no time together for fellowship to relax and enjoy one another's company. It was all hands on deck – all the time! It was wearing on us all. I finally told our small group, God gave us this ministry and I will continue until God takes it away even if I am the only one left. Our group eventually got down to about 6 adults working with the kids. Our whole church had good intentions but you know the old saying about good intentions being pavement for the highway to Hell. Jesus put it this way. *The spirit indeed is willing but the flesh is weak.* (Mat. 26:41) In the context of the scripture Jesus was telling the disciples to watch and pray. If you want to find out who is really serious about serving God have them watch and pray. If you want an better test, have them watch 45 rebellious kids! We started this ministry around 2016 and continued until COVID hit our area in the spring of 2020. When the Corona virus hit our nation, I couldn't help but think of Romans 8:28. *And we know that all things work together for good to those who love God, to those who are called according to His purpose.* Did I tell you it was a rough ministry? Though it was tough, those who stayed grew from it! I have always told our church that you don't always get to choose who you minister to. When God opens the door, by faith, walk through it!

If you want to follow Jesus to heaven, you had better start following him on earth. Jesus said, "*If anyone desires to come after me, let him deny himself, and take up his cross, and follow me.*" Following Jesus means to follow in his ways. Denying himself means putting the kingdom of God first and foremost. Taking up your cross is not bearing some irritating burden, but putting to death your own self interest and placing others first. It was not for Jesus' best interest to go to the cross; it was for yours. The only way you can follow Jesus is to put others first, even if it means crossing social and racial barriers. You have no scriptural basis for not crossing those barriers because they are only there in your mind. It is simply a matter of pride. Do not let pride keep you out of heaven. There is a celebration going on inside that you really do not want to miss.

Will jealousy leave you standing on the outside of heaven's gate refusing to enter? If Christ is truly in your heart and in your life, you should be filled with joy instead of jealousy. When sins are committed, there is no way to reverse the process or take them back. When an evil word is spoken, we may say, "I take it back," but in reality we cannot. It is done, and it cannot be undone. We cannot reel our words back in as if they were a fishing line. When an evil word is spoken, you can no more stop its effect than you can stop the effect on the water after a stone has been cast into a pond. You may not be able to stop the effect your sin has on others, but you can overcome the effect it will have on you by true heartfelt repentance. The Bible tells us in Luke, chapter 13, that unless we repent, we all shall perish. Admit you are wrong, and change your direction.

Every time we come under the conviction of the Holy Spirit about our sin and refuse to repent, the heart of our conscience becomes calloused and hardened. We are deceived into believing that our pride and jealousy can somehow be justified. It cannot, and there is no place for it in the house of God. *Exhort one another daily, while it is called today, lest any of you be hardened through the deceitfulness of sin.* (Heb. 3:13) Many churches today are filled with people professing to be Christians who are full of pride and jealousy, which will prevent them from entering heaven. Unfortunately, not only will they not enter, but they, like the elder son, will stand on the porch and block the entrance for others. We should be helping people out of the mud and slop of sin instead of ridiculing them for having been there. We should be helping to heal wounds instead of creating them. The elder brother in the parable was not happy with the return of the younger brother. It would have pleased him if the younger brother had never returned, and by the elder brother's attitude, he was probably happy when his brother left.

I have seen church members who were happy when someone broke fellowship with the congregation. The church body may have thought that anger was the reason they left. There is always someone who will give everyone his opinion of why the person left, but it is interesting to me that it is always someone who has not talked to those in question. Everyone assumes that those who left are the ones with the problem. They assume they know why they left; they assume they know how they feel, yet they never cared enough to go to the source and ask.

How would you feel if you lost an arm or leg? In what emotional state would you find yourself if you were to suddenly lose your sight or your hearing? Would you feel happy, joyful, or excited? I think not! Why then would a Christian express these emotions when part of the church body is no longer with them? When the church is happy because it has lost a member, there is a severe problem with the body. The body is certainly not following the head, which is Christ. The apostle Paul, speaking of Jesus in the book of Colossians, said, "*He is the head of the body, the church.*" (Col.1:18) People may think that it is all right to be happy when someone leaves because they feel the person leaving is wrong. Jesus was never happy about someone leaving or rejecting him even though they were wrong. As Jesus looked out over the city of Jerusalem, over those who rejected him, "*he saw the city and wept over it.*" (Luke 19:41) If the church is happy and Jesus is not, it may be that it is not the one who left who is rejecting Christ, but the church. Even if the church disagrees with someone, they should never rejoice when a person leaves the fellowship. As a pastor I have seen first hand, people join the church, say they are saved, show they have been baptized, and never show any evidence of being led by the Holy Spirit. They cause dissention and sow discord among the brethren. They refused to repent and would blame everyone around for problems they brought on themselves.

Eventually they would leave the church. Even then I was not happy that they left. I would prefer they repent, and allow God to change their lives. I was never happy when they left, but I must admit there were times when I was relieved!

The elder son might have been happy when the young son left; he was not happy when he returned. There was a celebration going on inside of the house. The elder son was standing on the outside refusing to go in. Where are you standing? Will you be close to the kingdom all your life and let jealousy, pride, and unforgiveness keep you from entering heaven, or will you repent and enter in?

Conclusion

According to the denomination to which you belong, you may have been taught different things from the parable of the prodigal son. If you were under the teaching of one denomination, you may have been taught that even though the younger son left his father's home and was living a life of sin, he was always the father's child, and, therefore, he represents the Christian who can never lose his salvation. Another denomination would teach the same scripture and tell you that the son was living in sin, out of the father's will, out of the father's life, and, therefore, if he had died in the hog pen he would spend an eternity in hell. They would say that he was saved when he was with the father and he lost his salvation when he left. When you have two opposing views, they cannot both be right. They can however both be wrong. We should never twist the scriptures in order to fit our Theology but let the scriptures determine our Theology.

We could say that we are all God's children by creation. The Bible tells us that God caused you to be conceived. God formed you in your mother's womb. He made you for a specific purpose and you are a wonder to behold. *For you formed my inward parts; You covered me in my mother's womb. I will praise you for I am fearfully and wonderfully made. Marvelous are your works.* (Ps. 139: 13-14) Though we may all be considered God's children by creation, we are not all God's children spiritually. Jesus said in John

8:44, *you are of your father the devil; and the desires of your father you want to do.* The young son had to get a new want to! The son's will had to get in line with God's will. He had to have a Garden of Gethsemane experience, where he was willing to say *not my will but thy will be done.* In order to change your want to, you have to have faith. There is no Justification without faith and there is no true faith without repentance. How can you honestly say you trust Jesus; how can you call Him Lord and not do as He says? Jesus said, *"But why do you call me "Lord, Lord," and not do the things which I say* (Lk 6:46) Jesus' first sermon was *repent for the kingdom of heaven is at hand,* (Mat. 4:17) and that is something we all must do. Jesus said in Luke 13:3 that *unless you repent you will all likewise perish.* Until the point of repentance (a changing of his mind that results in a change of action) there was no exhibit of faith and therefore there was no true faith. You might wonder how someone could make a statement like that. You might say, "You can't see what is in his heart". It is true we can't see his heart but we can see his actions. The young son Fred had made his own decision to leave the protection of the father. He had come to the age or point of accountability. He had gone against the father's will and was doing his own thing. Jesus puts it this way; *therefore by their fruits you will know them.* (Mat. 7:20

We can also know by reading and understanding the scripture. For instance, what do you call someone who has not placed their faith in Jesus for salvation? Answer: Lost! What call someone whose sins have not been forgiven? Answer: Lost! What do you call someone who is headed for an eternity in Hell? Answer: Lost or spiritually dead! Before we come to salvation we are also referred to as what? Answer: Lost or spiritually dead. What do you call someone who is constantly living in sin? Answer: Lost or spiritually dead! Now what would have happened if Fred had died in the pigpen? Let's look at the scripture again. *It was right that we should make merry and be glad, for your brother was dead and is alive again, and was lost and is found* (Luke15:32) Also read verse 24! *For this my son was dead and is alive again; he was lost and is found.* The words found in these two scriptures tell us where the young son was spiritually. We don't have to wonder, we are told in scripture. He was lost; he was spiritually dead. When he was in the pigpen, he was lost until he changed his mind (repented) and took the first step out of the pigpen and headed back to the father.

Throughout this book I have speculated about his desires, feelings, and reactions to the situation he found himself in. Whether or not these speculations were true about the son in the parable we may never know, but many were certainly true about this prodigal. I cannot tell you the exact moment when the son in the parable knew without a doubt that he had received salvation, but I can tell you when the Lord saved me. You may ask how you know for sure. That is easy! I was there when it happened. I did not walk an aisle, shake a preacher's hand, or get voted into a church. All of that had happened years earlier. I sat right there in the pew of a little Methodist church and received, by God's grace, the gift of salvation. It was not because of the church; I had never been there before, and I don't think I have ever been back again. It was not because of Methodist doctrine. It was not because of the Baptist evangelist that was preaching the revival. It wasn't the fact that that the evangelist had some Pentecostal ways and was more excited about Jesus than most all the Baptist or Methodist I had ever met. I couldn't even tell you what he said. It was simply listening to the Spirit of God speaking to me about my lack of trust in Him. God simply spoke to me and said, "If you really believed in me, you would be just as excited to tell others about me as this evangelist is". I knew it was the Holy Spirit speaking to me; I knew He was right, and I surrendered immediately. True faith, true belief, true trust produces surrender! Without moving a muscle, my heart was changed forever. *For by grace you have been saved through faith, and that not of yourselves; it is the gift of God.* (Eph. 2:8) Even though you may not have to move a muscle to receive salvation, I can assure you that after you have received it, you cannot continue to be satisfied just taking up pew space. When you become filled with the love of God, you just want to tell someone what God has done for you, and, for some reason, that will disturb the religious folks. My dear friend Andy Bryan explains this phenomenon in this way. These religious folk have spent a lot of time getting to know the word of God, but their problem is they do not know the God of the word. They know about God. They just do not know him. Just like the elder son in the parable, they have lived around the kingdom all their lives, yet they have never experienced the love and grace of God first hand, primarily because they have never admitted that they have been wrong. You cannot receive salvation without first admitting you are a sinner. *All we like sheep have gone astray; we have turned every one to his own way.* (Isaiah 53:6) You must first realize you are a prodigal before you can become a son.

We tend to think of this parable as being a story of one son who had wandered away and lived a life of sin, when actually it is a story of two sons who had wandered away. One wandered away literally, but they both had wandered away spiritually. We do know the one who left home, returned, and received forgiveness. The other one was left on the outside of the house, questioning the motives of the father.

I have seen many church members questioning the Father also. When they read the word of God and begin to feel uncomfortable, they will usually say something like, "I don't understand that," or "That is not really what that means." Some have even said, "I don't believe you should do that," or "That only happened in Jesus lifetime," even after it has been read straight from the word of God. The problem is that they have been taught and have believed many things that were not biblical. Isaiah prophesied about this, and Jesus reiterated it again in the gospel of Mark. *This people honors me with their lips, but their heart is far from me, and in vain they worship me, teaching as doctrines the commandments of men.* (Mark 7:6-7) Even though they would never admit it, many do question the word of God and the authority of God. That is why many people do not understand why some get so excited after surrendering their hearts and lives to Jesus Christ. It may be that the reason they do not understand it is because it has never happened to them. They are still standing on the porch refusing to go in. In order to believe in Christ or trust Christ, you must accept God's word and God's authority in your life without question.

When I repented of my sinful ways and trusted Jesus Christ as my Lord and Savior, it was then, and only then, that I could even begin to comprehend the love the Lord had for me. I was filled with a desire to tell others what God had done for you and me. I was also filled with the desire for all to live righteous, spirit-led lives. Do you have any idea what God has sacrificed for you? Do you desire to tell others what God has done in your life? Do you really want to know God even more? Do you desire to please Him? Do you desire that others receive that life changing relationship with the Savior? If not, maybe you claim to have accepted Christ, but since you do not trust Him enough to follow Him, He hasn't accepted you! We like the sound of it better if I accept Christ. We are in control. We want to take Jesus with us as our insurance policy while we live our lives the way we desire, but when Jesus calls us, He calls us to discipleship. He calls us to trust in Him, believe in Him, to the point that He becomes first in our lives above all else. *Jesus said to His disciples, "If anyone desires to come after Me, let him deny himself, and take up his cross, and follow me.* (Mat. 16:24) We must admit our faults and allow God to perform spiritual surgery on our hearts. God can do this, but we must sign the consent form of repentance. Then Jesus will accept us and give us the grace to enable us to follow Him.

If I ever have the opportunity to minister to you in some way, and you feel that I am beating you up with scripture or preaching down to you, please understand that it may not be me that is making you feel uncomfortable. It may be that the Holy Spirit would like your permission to do a little heart surgery. Sign the permission slip of repentance. I guarantee the Holy Spirit's heart surgery will never leave a scar. He does not just repair it; he returns it to its original state. He wants to restore you, not patch you up. He will not do bypass surgery; he will restore your heart by removing the carnality and replacing the spirituality.

Jesus loves us so much that he gave his life for us. In the day that we live, most people love you when it is convenient, or if you are in agreement with them. God loves us even when we oppose him. *But God demonstrates his own love toward us, in that while we were still sinners, Christ died for us.* (Rom. 5:8) There are many who say, "I believe in Jesus". They may say that they believe Jesus is the Son of God, that He lived a sinless life, that He cast out demons and healed people, that He died on the cross for the sins of the world and rose the third day. All that is good and you should believe that, but that won't get you into heaven! You see, Satan and all his followers believe that. They not only believe it – they know it – they were there when it happened. When Jesus healed the demon possessed man, the demons within him cried out, *"What have I to do with you Jesus, Son of the Most High God? I beg you do not torment me!"* (Lk. 8:28) The demons don't just believe, they know who Jesus is, but they refuse to live for him.

Jesus loved you enough to give his life for you. Could you love him enough that it would affect the way you live yours?

If you were to examine your life, you would find that there is some part in this parable that would exemplify your life. Where do you belong in the parable? Are you beginning to wander away from God? Are you in the pigpen of sin? Have you come home to experience the grace and forgiveness of God? Have you been hanging around the kingdom all your life, never receiving the blessings God has for you? Will you come to the entrance of heaven itself and let pride, resentment, and unforgiveness prevent you from entering? Will you admit that you are a prodigal so you may become a son, or will you be left standing on the porch when the door of heaven is shut? It is all up to you. God has made the provision for you to enter. There is only one requirement that you must meet. Repent (change direction) and trust Jesus Christ (follow him) —God's provision for you. The choice is yours. Which will it be?

Where will you go from here?

So you have left the sinful life behind and you are now proclaiming God's grace to all who will listen. You have made it from the pigpen to the pulpit, but will you go beyond? Statistics are against you! You're thinking, I have finally arrived; and in a way, you have, but not to your final destination. You have now arrived to the battle field. You are now on the front lines. You will be in a daily battle with the world, the flesh, and the devil. You now have a target on your back. The principalities, powers, and darkness that we wrestle against were not your enemies when you were following the world. Now they will be working to take you out. Many come out of the gate strong, but how many will finish. God's Word gives us a hint with the biggest three letter word in the Bible. Few! *Because narrow is the gate and difficult is the way which leads to life, and there are few who find it.* (Mat. 7:14) Many will fall by the wayside. Many will compromise. Many will tire of the difficulty and choose the easy route. Many who fall will just stay down rather than get up and get back in the battle. It will be too hard for them because they are trying to fight the battle on their own and this battle was never meant to be fought that way. I have asked people if they were a Christian and they would respond, "I'm Trying". I always tell them to stop trying and start trusting! This battle is not won by your efforts but by your faith! How do you win a battle by faith? **F**orsaking **A**ll **I** **T**rust **H**im! Faith in Him means following Him! No matter what you think, no matter how you feel! It is not about your intelligence or your feelings; it's about following! It is about your obedience to the one you call Lord and Master! If He is not your Lord and Master He is not your Savior! Nowhere in the Bible does it say Christ can be your savior and not your lord. It always says Savior and Lord. He is only Savior of those who look to Him as Lord and if He is Lord then He calls the shots!

You do not have to perform or reach a goal. You don't get punished, or demoted if you don't get the results you hoped for. God just wants your trust, and you show that by your obedience, no matter the results. Just follow! *For as many as are led by the Spirit of God, these are the sons of God.* (Rom. 8:14)

In order to stay in the battle, you need to study His Word, and meditate on His Word. Sin can take you out of the battle and you may never reach the final destination. *Your word I have hidden in my heart that I might not sin against you.* (Ps. 119:11)

In this battle and on this journey there will be many blessings that may come your way. There will be things that God will show you to strengthen you for battle and encourage you to keep going. There will be conformation given to you so you will know you are on the right path. This is God's sanctifying grace to keep you going during the every day drudgery of the journey just because He is a good God and wants to strengthen and encourage you.

There will be times when major battles will arise. They may be battles in your own life or they may be battles just for what is right. During these times God will require something of you. There may be certain criteria that must be met before God will act and He will not act until this criterion is met. 2 Ch. 7:14 is an example. *If my people who are called by my name will humble themselves, and pray, and seek my face, and turn from their wicked ways, then I will hear from heaven, and will forgive their sin and heal their land.* In order for sin to be forgiven for a nation, God's people must humble themselves, pray, seek the Lord, and repent of their sins. God's people must not think more highly of themselves than they ought. We are all sinners saved by grace. We must go to God in prayer on a regular basis, not to ask for something we want, but to hear what He wants. We must put our relationship with Him above all else. We must get to know His ways. When we know His ways, we may then turn from our wicked ways to His Holy ways.

This battle field, this journey we are on, is what we call salvation! Salvation is not saying a prayer, shaking the preachers' hand, getting dunked in the baptismal waters, or voted into a church. It is a daily walk with Jesus Christ from the day you say yes to Him until you breathe your last breath on this earth. It's not a one and done kind of deal. It is about being a disciple of Christ. When Jesus called people to believe on Him, He was calling them to discipleship. Believe in Him enough to follow Him. The call is the same today! There is no salvation without discipleship!

Many will blame God for the difficulties that come their way because they were told by some prosperity hustler, I mean preacher (and I use the word preacher very loosely here) that after you become a Christian everything would be wonderful. The Bible says that *difficult is the way*. It is wonderful but it is not easy. It is wonderful because you now no longer have to be good enough to get to heaven, just follow the one who knows the way. It is wonderful because you get to see God do awesome things along the way, but many won't see it because they have stepped off the path that God has for them. They are not following God so they are not in the position to see God working up ahead of them preparing the way when there seems to be no way. They won't recognize how God works through others around them, and they will never experience the power of God as He works through them. Obedience is the key to seeing and experiencing God at work!

Throughout God's word God has told us that salvation is about continuing on the journey, staying with the plan, remaining with Him, no matter what obstacles may get in our way. If you fall, repent, get back on track, and stay the course. *Repent and do the first works or I will come quickly and remove your lampstand.* (Rev. 2:5) Keep going, don't quit! *If you continue in my word then you are my disciples.* (John 8:31) You are not a disciple because you said a prayer once; you are a disciple because you continue! *Continue in my love.* (John 15:9) *Continue in the grace of God.* (Acts 13:43) *Continue in the faith* (Acts 14:22) It doesn't mean you will live a perfect life without ever sinning but it does mean that no matter what obstacles you may face God will help you overcome if you continue! When we fail, when we fall, repent. Luther said that the Christian life is a life of repentance! That is how you continue; that is how you overcome. *He who overcomes/I will give a new name* (Rev. 2:17) *He who overcomes and keeps my works until the end, to him I will give power over the nations.* (Rev. 2:26) *He who overcomes shall be clothed in white garments* (Rev. 3:5) *He who overcomes I will make him a pillar in the temple of God.* (Rev. 3:12) *He who overcomes I will grant to sit with me on my throne.* (Rev. 3:21) In order to continue this journey, to be effective ambassadors for Christ, and overcome all obstacles that may get in our way, we must get close, and remain close to Christ! *He who abides in Me and I in him bears much fruit for without me you can do nothing.* (John

15:5) In this context, Jesus is saying we must remain close to him, receive our nourishment, and sustenance from Him. We also have a warning from Christ if we fail to abide. *If anyone does not abide in Me, he is cast out as a branch and is withered; and they gather them and throw them into the fire, and they are burned.* (John 15:6) In short, if we abide, continue, remain, and overcome we will finish the journey of Salvation to our heavenly home. In order to overcome we have to stick with Jesus! We are preserved by grace! We are saved by grace! We grow by grace, and we will be glorified by grace! If we fail to stay with Jesus, we will miss God's grace, and will forever be in a battlefield of the mind and soul called Hell, *where the worm does not die and the fire is not quenched.* (Mk. 8:44, 46, 48)

At this point in my life, I have gone from the pigpen to the pulpit, God is still working on me, and I am looking forward to the Beyond!

You are in a battle, but the war is already won! Abide – Remain – Continue – Overcome; it can only be done by following Jesus as the Holy Spirit leads! I look forward to seeing you in THE BEYOND!

Romans 8:14 For as many as are led by the Spirit of God, these are the Son's of God!

Thank you for taking the time to read this book. I know this book was written under the power of the Holy Spirit because the wording of the content is beyond my natural ability. I pray that in some way it has touched your heart, enlightened your mind and will give you the strength to continue, remain, abide, and over come!

May God richly bless you!

CPSIA information can be obtained
at www.ICGtesting.com
Printed in the USA
LVHW040631310522
720059LV00005B/79

9 781662 849916